BUILDING VOCABULARY

with Greek & Latin Roots

2nd Edition

A Professional Guide to Word Knowledge and Vocabulary Development

Timothy
Rasinski, Ph.D.

Nancy
Padak, Ed.D.

Rick M.
Newton, Ph.D.

Evangeline
Newton, Ph.D.

**Forewords by Chase Young
and Karen Bromley**

Contributing Author

Joanna Newton, Ph.D., Fairfax County Public Schools, Virginia

Publishing Credits

Corinne Burton, M.A.Ed., *Publisher*
Aubrie Nielsen M.S.Ed., *EVP of Content Development*
Véronique Bos, *Creative Director*
Shaun N. Bernadou, *Art Director*
Noelle Cristea, M.A.Ed., *Senior Editor*
John Leach, *Assistant Editor*
Julie Guzman, *Digital Producer*
Kevin Pham, *Design Lead*

Image Credits

All images from iStock and/or Shutterstock.

A division of Teacher Created Materials
5482 Argosy Avenue
Huntington Beach, CA 92649-1039
www.tcmpub.com/shell-education
978-0-7439-1643-1
© 2020 Shell Education Publishing, Inc.

Table of Contents

Chapter 10: The Story of English—How Did We Get Here?

Appendices

Forewords

Having used the first edition of this book with my students for years, I can tell you firsthand that students actually begin to view themselves as geniuses (and rightly so) as they identify words based on Greek and Latin roots. For example, they learn that *val* means "strong," and they are elated when they find the root in other words: *valiant*, *valor*, *validate*, and *valedictorian*.

So, be prepared for your students to emphatically notify you (repeatedly!) when they find a newly learned Greek or Latin root in the context of their reading, and remember it is a good thing—your students are excited about vocabulary! Arguably, if you can get them to like learning new words, your job is practically done; students will pay more attention to new and unfamiliar words in their reading, and they will likely attempt to understand those words all on their own. Remember, the job of a teacher is making oneself progressively unnecessary.

The second edition of *Building Vocabulary with Greek and Latin Roots* has even more to offer teachers, reading specialists, curriculum coordinators, and others who are charged with the difficult task of vocabulary instruction. Much like the first edition, this text is reader friendly, provides useful insights about planning instruction,

and—my favorite—includes ideas for having fun while playing with words. There are several features of this new edition that are worth noting. First, like a dedicated group of educators, the authors updated the instructional frameworks and activities to reflect the most recent research on vocabulary instruction. In addition, they show how to help students "flex" with words by understanding that the same word can have multiple meanings ("vanilla *extract*" and "*extract* a tooth") and both a literal and a figurative meaning ("*extract* a tooth" and "*extract* the truth"). This edition also provides considerations for the youngest of students, diverse learners, those who need creative extensions, and those learning English. For teachers curious about how this type of vocabulary program actually plays out in the classroom, there's an entire chapter devoted to just that. These additions, and many others, make the second edition an even stronger tool to guide your vocabulary instruction.

The power of knowing roots came home to me not long ago, when I visited a private preschool in Texas. I sat in a circle with three- and four-year-olds for a science lesson. Naturally, I sat next to the most energetic boy in the bunch—it's my comfort zone. The lesson was on viviparous animals. The teacher began by showing flashcards of animals, and students either exclaimed "viviparous" or "oviparous." Admittedly, I had no idea what was going on. I asked the fidgety genius next to me, and he clued me in: "Mister, viviparous animals have live babies, and oviparous animals lay eggs." Because of his tone, I halfway expected him to end his explanation with a sarcastic "Duh!" I was a bit ashamed, and the teacher politely helped me understand the Latin roots: *viv* means "alive," *ovo* means "egg," and *parus* means "bearing." It all made sense. At that point, I was able to join the rest of the group by viewing myself as a genius.

Chase Young, Ph.D.
Associate Professor
School of Teaching and Learning
Sam Houston State University

As I began to read this book, the phrase that caught my eye was "divide and conquer." What better way is there to help teachers and students at all grade levels learn how to make sense of difficult, multisyllabic words than by dissecting them? *Building Vocabulary with Greek and Latin Roots* is a book that does just this. It shows us how to help students understand the meanings of word parts in order to learn new words. This book is an invaluable resource for classroom teachers, content-area teachers, reading specialists, staff developers, curriculum coordinators, and lovers of language. It provides us with important understandings about the English language that most of us did not grow up with and may not have acquired in our schooling.

Did you know that 90 percent of English words with more than one syllable are Latin based and most of the remaining 10 percent are Greek based? Did you know that a single root can help us understand 5 to 20 related English words? *Building Vocabulary with Greek and Latin Roots* is packed with this kind of information. Because the English language and the content areas contain so many multisyllabic and technical words, teachers of language arts, science, social studies, and mathematics will find this book particularly helpful in supporting their students as they learn to discern word meanings.

Several aspects of this easy-to-read book also caught my eye, making it a valuable addition to my teaching library. First, it provides a synopsis of the theory and research that support teaching multisyllabic words by dissecting roots (prefixes, bases, and suffixes). Second, the book offers ideas for planning vocabulary instruction and includes activities, such as Word Spokes, Wordo, Scattergories, and Making and Writing Words, to engage students in actively understanding roots as they become independent word learners. Third, the book includes valuable resources, such as extensive lists of commonly taught roots and their meanings, professional resources for teachers, websites, dictionaries, and sources for lesson plans. Finally, as I stopped to reflect at the end of each chapter, it occurred to me that this book is a good resource for a teachers' study group. It is well worth the time spent reading and discussing with colleagues because the ideas it holds are basic to rethinking and transforming vocabulary instruction.

The information in *Building Vocabulary with Greek and Latin Roots* is critical to being a good vocabulary teacher at all grade levels. I believe the authors have written a terrific book that can help classroom teachers, content-area teachers, reading specialists, staff developers, curriculum coordinators, and lovers of language as they support students in learning how to "divide and conquer" multisyllabic words.

Karen Bromley, Ph.D.
Distinguished Teaching Professor Emerita
Graduate School of Education
Binghamton University
State University of New York

Preface to the Second Edition

In the introduction to the first edition of this book, we asked our readers about a new word: *locavore*. We asked them to guess what this word meant and to speculate about the clues you might use to figure it out. *Locavore* was one of 10 buzzwords of 2007, according to *Time* magazine (Cruz 2007).

Language changes! What was a brand-new word a few years ago is now in common usage. This is just one of the many challenges associated with vocabulary instruction: language is fluid, and vocabulary is dynamic. Other challenges abound: Which words should we teach? How can we best teach them? How can we make sure we reach all learners? These are important questions, for we know that good vocabulary instruction will support much of the other learning students do in school. This is why we have written a second edition.

In these pages, you will find research-based practices that can help your students develop their vocabularies. Throughout, we emphasize using word roots (prefixes, suffixes, and bases) as an efficient and effective way to build vocabulary and word awareness. For example, even the new word *locavore* is built on the Latin bases *vor* ("eat") and *loc* ("place"). The awareness of how words work from a roots approach is an invaluable asset for lifelong learning.

In the second edition, we incorporate the latest research in morphological vocabulary instruction, underscoring the importance of teaching word patterns. We present updated instructional models and strategies from a roots perspective, drawing on the experience of teachers who use this approach. We also highlight differentiation strategies, including suggestions for assisting English learners, particularly those who speak Spanish. Moreover, we have added two new chapters. One provides guidelines on how to move beginning and early readers from sound to meaning patterns. The other explains how "spelling matters" can be used in vocabulary instruction, offering useful tips on connecting correct spelling with correct meaning. Finally, we have updated appendices of additional resources for students and teachers.

We are grateful for the scores of teachers who have shared their vocabulary instruction stories with us over the years. This book reflects all their suggestions. We particularly thank Dr. Joanna Newton, who has taught and supported the implementation of roots-based vocabulary practices in many classrooms. Insights from her work with teachers as a literacy specialist and through professional development workshops are integral to this book.

Our instructional series *Building Vocabulary* details yearlong word-learning routines for students in grades K–11. If you are using the *Building Vocabulary* curriculum in your classroom, this book will provide you with adaptations that you and your students will find beneficial. You will find many references to the series, as the updates made there are reflected in theory and practice in this second edition. Alternatively, if you are using another vocabulary series (or none at all), this book will provide new insights against which you can evaluate your current program or develop a new one. Happy reading!

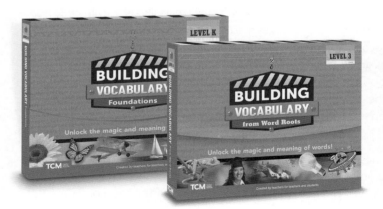

Available for purchase at **www.teachercreatedmaterials.com**

CHAPTER 1

Teaching Vocabulary: What Does the Research Say?

Have you ever visited the National World War II Museum in New Orleans? It is a fascinating place. Among the documents available for viewing is the first draft of President Franklin Delano Roosevelt's famous speech that begins "Yesterday, December 7, 1941—a date which will live in *infamy*." These powerful words helped the nation prepare for war. But they were not the first words FDR wrote. The first draft of the beginning of the speech reads "a date which will live in *world history*." Which do you think is more memorable, "infamy" or "world history"?

Word choice really does make a difference. Mark Twain once observed that "the difference between the almost right word and the right word is really a large matter—

it is the difference between the lightning bug and the lightning." This book is all about helping students find and use the right words.

As every teacher knows, this is no small task. The English language has approximately two million words! And every year, technological advances bring us new modes of communication—and new words. One estimate is that technology is contributing about 20,000 words per year to our language. What are teachers to do?

Until very recently, most formal vocabulary instruction has been limited to a few strategies. Students have often been asked to learn the meanings of words by finding and memorizing definitions. Students have also been introduced to new words before reading a story or told to pay special attention to boldface words in their content-area texts. But just relying on these approaches to build vocabulary does not work. In fact, results of national assessments of 4th, 8th, and 12th grade students' vocabulary development confirm what we already knew: students have demonstrated no improvement in vocabulary knowledge since 2009 (National Center for Education Statistics 2015). And during the same period, reading achievement has been stagnant as well. As educators, we must do more.

How can we—and students—ever catch up? Luckily, there is a way. Consider this: 90 percent of English words with more than one syllable are Latin based. Most of the remaining 10 percent are Greek based (Brunner 2004). A single Latin root generates five or more English words.

According to Graves and Fitzgerald (2006), school texts and reading materials include more than 180,000 different words. Since most of the words found in these texts come to English from Greek and Latin roots, knowledge of these word parts is a powerful tool in unlocking the complex vocabulary of mathematics, science, literature, and social studies. In addition, most of those 20,000 new "technology" words we mentioned are derived from Greek or Latin. Did you know, for example, that a computer *cursor* and a race *course* both come from the Latin verb *curro*, "to run"?

Today, many students come to our classrooms speaking languages that are largely derived from Latin, such as Spanish. In fact, about 75 percent of the Spanish language is descended from Latin (Chandler and Schwartz 1961). Students who come to school with Spanish as a first language can easily make connections between Spanish and English because the two languages share many cognate words (i.e., words with a common origin). Building vocabulary by learning how to apply the meaning of Greek and Latin word roots can help all students, including those who are learning English.

Moreover, using roots to unlock word meanings will do more than expand students' vocabularies. Each word built from roots has taken a unique path into our language. Did you know, for example, that the words *vocabulary* and *vowel* come from the Latin root *voc*, which means "voice"? In ancient Rome, students were required to recite lists of new words orally, or using their "voices." And of course, we need our "voices" to say "*a, e, i, o, u*." Studying word roots may start your students on a fascinating exploration of word histories. Just as important, it will help students grasp an essential linguistic principle: English words have a discernible logic because their meanings are historically grounded. This knowledge—used in conjunction with word-analysis skills—empowers students as learners.

The ability for students to think critically is inextricably tied to how much knowledge they have about the topic (Wexler 2019). Although no single approach to vocabulary development has been found conclusively to be more successful than another, researchers agree that a focus on Greek and Latin derivatives offers a powerful tool for teachers to nurture students' vocabulary development (Bear et al. 2000; Blachowicz and Fisher 2002, 2006; Newton, Padak, and Rasinski 2008; Rasinski and Padak 2013; Rasinski, Padak, and Newton 2017; Stahl 1986, 1992). A focus on how words work and providing students with the tools that unlock language is what this book is all about. In this chapter, we begin our study of roots by addressing two broad and critical issues: why vocabulary is important and what we know about effective instruction. We will then offer some insights into vocabulary instruction for English learners (ELs).

Importance of Vocabulary in Literacy Development

Vocabulary is knowledge of word meanings. The simplicity of this definition does not quite convey what it means to "know" a word. For example, *Merriam-Webster's Collegiate Dictionary* lists 18 definitions (several of them with subdefinitions) for the word *place*. Although we rarely stop to think about it, the issue of knowing words is complex.

Nagy and Scott (2000) have helped us understand the complexity of what it means to know a word. They argue that word knowledge has at least five different components or aspects:

- Incrementality—Each time we encounter a new word, our knowledge of its definition(s) and possible uses becomes a bit more precise, showing that word knowledge is incremental. Think about how your own understanding of familiar words, such as *love* or *free*, has deepened over time. As Pearson, Hiebert, and Kamil note, "knowing a word is not an all-or-nothing matter" (2007, 286).

- Multidimensionality—Word knowledge extends beyond simple definitions. It can include subtle conceptual differences between synonyms. For example, both *allege* and *believe* share a core meaning of "certainty" or "conviction." Yet they are conceptually distinct. I may *believe* I saw a flying saucer in the sky, but if I report it to the police, they will probably call my sighting an *alleged* event. Why? How are the two words different? Collocation, or the frequent placing together of words, is also a part of word knowledge. We can talk about a *storm front*, but not a *storm back* (Pearson, Hiebert, and Kamil 2007). Similarly, we can have a *storm door* and a *storm window*, but not a *storm ceiling* or a *storm floor*.

- Polysemy—Many words, especially common ones, have multiple meanings. Depending on the context in which it is used, sometimes the same word can have either a literal or a figurative meaning. Knowing those multiple meanings is part of knowing the words. Think about the different contexts and ways in which the word *place* can be used. An outdoor grocery store can be called a *marketplace*, while a horse that *places* finishes a race in second place. And remember Dorothy in *The Wizard of Oz*? She reminds us "there's no *place* like home."

- Interrelatedness—Knowing a word often involves knowing its attributes and how it is related to other words or concepts. Think of all the things you know about even a simple word such as *rat*, and you will quickly see this aspect of interrelatedness in action.

- Heterogeneity—Again using *place* as an example, consider that a word's meaning is dependent on its context, both semantic and syntactic.
  - Her ideas were all over the *place*.
  - In gym class, we had to run in *place*.
  - This weekend, we will go to our summer *place*.

These examples demonstrate that there is nothing simple about knowing a word. As Pearson, Hiebert, and Kamil note, "Words may seem like simple entities, but they are not. Their surface simplicity belies a deeper complexity" (2007, 286).

Vocabulary and Reading Comprehension

Furthermore, no teacher will be surprised to learn that decades of research have consistently found a deep and complex connection between vocabulary knowledge, reading comprehension, and academic success (Baumann, Kame'enui, and Ash 2003). Amazingly, upwards of 80 percent of students' reading comprehension test scores can be accounted for by vocabulary knowledge (Reutzel and Cooter 2015). The larger a reader's vocabulary, the easier it is for them to understand the meaning of a text (National

Reading Panel 2000). Widely accepted is the understanding that students with less overall knowledge and breadth of vocabulary are always at a disadvantage (Wexler 2019).

One aspect of the vocabulary comprehension complexity is seen in the word knowledge that students bring to the classroom. Each of us has an active vocabulary and a passive vocabulary. An active vocabulary includes words that we can quickly generate for speaking or writing because we know them well. We can recognize words in our passive vocabulary when we encounter them; but we do not regularly use them. Think back to FDR's speech. Chances are we understood what FDR meant by "infamy" because we have seen it in other contexts. Yet, when is the last time you used this word in a sentence? One goal of vocabulary instruction is to increase both active and passive vocabularies. This goal is critical because research has shown that students who begin school with smaller vocabularies remain at an academic disadvantage throughout their schooling (Hart and Risley 1995, 2003).

Did You Know?

Spoken language is socially contextualized. In conversation, for example, we use gestures to help convey meaning. The participants in a conversation can ask for clarification. Written language, on the other hand, tends to be socially decontextualized, so precision of word choice is very important. (The writer may not be readily available to clarify a text's meaning.) Most of the new vocabulary students encounter in school is through reading written texts, and much of it is decontextualized.

The social context in which words are encountered provides yet another layer of complexity. We use oral vocabulary to listen and speak, and print vocabulary to read and write. Spoken language is socially contextualized. In conversation, for example, we use gestures to help convey meaning. The participants in a conversation can ask for clarification. Written language, on the other hand, tends to be socially decontextualized, so precision of word choice is very important. (The writer may not be readily available to clarify a text's meaning.) Most of the new vocabulary students encounter in school is through reading written texts, and much of it is decontextualized.

Kamil and Hiebert describe vocabulary as a bridge between the "word-level processes of phonics and the cognitive processes of comprehension" (2005, 4). This is a useful way to visualize the importance of vocabulary for young readers. A solid bank of conceptual knowledge is essential for reading because it facilitates word identification and enables comprehension. But meaning does not automatically follow successful decoding. If a word is not in a child's oral vocabulary, the child cannot apply word recognition strategies effectively, and reading comprehension is hindered (National Reading Panel 2000). Wide conceptual knowledge supports decoding. An extensive vocabulary helps students read fluently, comprehend, discuss what they have read, and learn.

The Vocabulary of School

A central goal of vocabulary instruction, then, is to expand students' conceptual knowledge. In school, this means expanding what we call *academic vocabulary*. Academic vocabulary consists of words and phrases students must understand to grasp critical content-area concepts (Baumann and Graves 2010) and to participate successfully in classroom learning (Bravo and Cervetti 2008). Consider this: if we were reading a bedtime story at home, we might ask our children to *guess* what the ending will be. If we were reading that same book to our students, however, we would ask them to *predict* the ending. According to *Merriam-Webster*, *guessing* and *predicting* are synonyms that involve the same basic concept of "estimating." But unlike a guess, a prediction is a confident and thought-out declaration that is "spoken" (*dict–*) "before" (*pre–*) a final outcome. *Guess* is what we do at home; *predict* is what we do at school. Of these two words, *predict* is Latin based and *guess* is not.

Most students come to us with an understanding of the word *guess*. Many students may also come to us with an understanding of the concept *estimate*. Our job is to help them build on what they already know to learn the academic word *predict*.

Scholars have identified four broad categories of academic vocabulary to keep in mind as we plan instruction (Hiebert and Lubliner 2008). Students need proficiency with each to be successful in school.

1. **Task-Specific Vocabulary**—Task-specific vocabulary refers to the language that students must understand in order to complete school assignments. These can be commonplace terms, such as *reading log, vocabulary journal, preview*, or *summarize*. They can also be content-specific terms, such as *hypothesize, conclude, classify*, or *observe*. Students' task-specific vocabulary knowledge affects performance on comprehension tasks (Cunningham and Moore 1993) and achievement tests (Butler, Stevens, and Castellon 2007).

2. **Content-Specific Vocabulary**—Content-specific vocabulary represents concepts that are integral to a field of study (e.g., *photosynthesis* and *chlorophyll* in science, *perimeter* and *integer* in mathematics, *symbolism* and *metaphor* in reading). Many content-specific vocabulary words are abstract and decontextualized and are encountered most frequently in written form.

   Content-specific vocabulary can be challenging for students because it involves learning new words for new ideas (Harmon, Wood, and Hedrick 2008). Since content-specific vocabulary occurs infrequently outside school, it is unlikely that students will learn the words indirectly (Worthington and Nation 1996). When students acquire the vocabulary of a discipline, they learn the concepts and relationships among concepts that comprise the discipline (Bravo and Cervetti 2008). Limited understanding of content-specific vocabulary not only leads to misconceptions and gaps in learning, but it may also hinder future learning, since students build new understandings on existing knowledge (Blachowicz and Obrochta 2005).

3. **Literary Vocabulary**—Literary vocabulary refers to words and phrases students encounter when reading literature. Most literary vocabulary is not in students' active vocabularies. Moreover, literary vocabulary sometimes involves shades of meaning; authors might use words such as *bliss* or *elation* as synonyms for *joy*, for example. Understanding the importance of these nuances of meaning may add to students' challenges when reading.

4. **General Academic Vocabulary**—General academic vocabulary appears frequently across academic areas but is not content specific. These words are challenging because they can assume multiple meanings across various contexts (Bravo and Cervetti 2008). For example, consider *revolution* in science and social studies or *movement* in social studies, science, music, or physical education. To deal with general academic vocabulary successfully, students must recognize the intended meaning of the words within the appropriate contexts.

In all, the decontextualized language of school texts contains richer vocabulary and more unfamiliar words than spoken language (Cunningham 2005). Content-area vocabulary is abstract, technical, and assumes multiple meanings in various contexts—all of this adds cognitive complexity to reading and learning. To learn the infrequently used words that will help students comprehend increasingly complex school texts, they need multiple opportunities to experience words in both oral and written contexts.

You may agree with us that this is a daunting task. For example, although most researchers believe that students naturally add between 2,000 and 3,000 new words each year, Nagy and Anderson (1984) estimate that fifth graders encounter 10,000 new words each year in their reading alone. Fortunately, more than 4,000 of the new words that fifth graders encounter are derivatives of familiar words—most of them of Greek or Latin origin (usually compound words and words with prefixes and suffixes). In fact, well over half of English words—nearly 75 percent (and more than 90 percent of words with more than one syllable) according to some estimates—are derived from Greek or Latin. This is another reason why a focus on word parts makes sense as part of a vocabulary program.

The Roots Advantage

Greek and Latin prefixes, bases, and suffixes are fairly consistent in their meanings and spelling patterns. Consequently, students can figure out the pronunciation and meaning of many new words by looking at their roots. They will understand the logic in the spelling pattern. A student who knows that the root *spec, spect* means "look," for example, has a head start in figuring out what *speculate, spectacular,* and *spectacle* mean when encountering them in a text. The student can then use context to determine whether the *spectacle* in question is a "big event" or, when used in the plural form, a "pair of glasses." This clear link among pronunciation, meaning, and spelling is especially useful for young readers because they are able to coordinate sound and sense when they encounter new and challenging words (Bear et al. 2000; Rasinski and Padak 2013). And as students move from grade to grade, they face an increased number of new words, new concepts, and multiple meanings (Blachowicz and Fisher 2015). Fortunately, knowledge of roots and the ability to "look inside" unfamiliar words for meaning can help students conquer some of this academic challenge.

The study of word roots also provides a smooth and natural continuum or bridge for students in their study of words. In the primary grades, word study is generally focused more on the letter-sound relationships in words (phonics and spelling). One of the most productive ways of teaching letter-sound relationships is through word families, or rimes. A word family is a sound-based word pattern that can help readers decode and spell many words. For example, knowing the sounds represented by the word family *–ack* allows students to decode and spell words such as *back, crack, jack, lack, pack, rack, sack, stack,* and *shack*. Roots, too, are word patterns. However, in addition to representing the *sounds* embedded in words, roots also represent the *meaning* embedded in words. The study of roots for vocabulary building, then, can be a natural transition for students who have been taught phonics and spelling using word families.

We hope that this brief research review has convinced you that effective vocabulary instruction with Greek and Latin roots has the potential to foster students' literacy learning. Unfortunately, at present there is little classroom-based research that provides descriptions of effective vocabulary instruction in practice. Sweet and Snow (2003), reporting on results from the RAND Reading Study Group's examination of comprehension, note that the number of studies examining the effect of vocabulary instruction on reading comprehension has been small. Similarly, the NRP noted that research on vocabulary acquisition greatly "exceeds current knowledge of pedagogy" and cited a "great need" for research on this topic "in authentic school contexts, with real teachers, under real conditions" (2000, 4).

Sadly, this is still true. Despite the lack of classroom-based studies, however, research has conclusively demonstrated the need for comprehensive vocabulary instruction and word study curricula (Blachowicz et al. 2006). In the next section, we offer general principles for designing vocabulary instruction.

Five Principles for Word Learning

Until recently, most formal vocabulary instruction has been limited to the introduction of key words before reading a new text. According to vocabulary scholar Margaret McKeown, very little vocabulary instruction happens in many U.S. classrooms (Banchero 2013). Where vocabulary instruction does occur, students often come to view it as painful and meaningless: weekly lists of words, memorized definitions and spellings, and quizzes. Students may memorize words and definitions, but these are quickly forgotten. The result of either approach—benign neglect or rote memorization—is stagnation in our students' vocabulary knowledge.

Although researchers agree on the curricular importance of vocabulary instruction, guidance about instructional methodology is still in early stages. Kamil and Hiebert (2005) identify four core unresolved instructional issues that have serious implications for lesson planning:

1. How many words should be taught?

2. Which words should be taught?

3. How should we teach students for whom reading is difficult and/or English is a new language?

4. How does independent reading support vocabulary learning?

Despite these ongoing issues, researchers have begun to provide instructional guidance in vocabulary acquisition. For example, Biemiller (2005, 225) argues that even different student populations learn words "largely in the same order" and calls for teaching a corpus of common word roots, even in primary grades. Blachowicz and Fisher (2015) believe that two decades of research on vocabulary acquisition can be summarized into four broad instructional principles:

- Students should develop an understanding of words and ways to learn them through active engagement.

- Students should personalize word learning to make personal connections by drawing on what they already know to understand what they do not know.

- Students should be immersed in words.

- Students should experience repeated exposures by accessing words through multiple sources of information.

Researchers also agree that no single instructional method is sufficient to enhance students' vocabularies. Teachers need a variety of methods that teach word meanings while increasing the depth of word knowledge (Blachowicz et al. 2006; Lehr, Osborn, and Hiebert 2004). Five principles can be used to select, evaluate, or create effective vocabulary instruction:

1. Instruction should include *planned teaching* of selected words with multiple kinds of information provided (e.g., semantic, structural) (Blachowicz et al. 2006). Research tells us that students can only learn 8–10 new words each week through direct instruction (Stahl and Fairbanks 1986). Some direct instruction is useful.

2. Vocabulary instruction should be *integrative* (Nagy 1988). To learn new words—really learn them—requires students to connect new and existing knowledge. Words are best learned when presented meaningfully with attention to definitions (Nagy 1988; Stahl 1986). Students need to use new words in meaningful contexts and think about them in meaningful ways. Attention to definitions adds power to this word learning (Stahl and Fairbanks 1986). Teachers must find ways to focus on connections between what students already know and words they are going to learn. Activities that ask students to explore similarities and differences among concepts, activate background knowledge, and generate and test hypotheses seem particularly beneficial (Blachowicz and Fisher 2015; Marzano, Pickering, and Pollock 2001).

3. Vocabulary instruction needs to include repetition (Blachowicz and Fisher 2015; Nagy 1988; Stahl 1986). Students should be *immersed* in words, with frequent opportunities to encounter and use new words in diverse oral and print contexts to learn them on a deep level. Research tells us that we learn more new words incidentally, when they occur in our reading or listening, than we do through direct instruction (Lehr, Osborn, and Hiebert 2004).

   Teacher read-alouds can help students develop vocabulary, especially if the books have wonderful words and powerful language. If students will be tackling a new or difficult concept in the content areas, read-alouds could include picture books or other texts that address the topic. Related to this principle is another: the importance of students' wide reading. The more students read, the better. Using new words in discussion and writing also facilitates their learning. In fact, we recommend that you challenge students to use new words in as many ways as possible.

4. Word learning is a procedural activity—a matter of knowing *how*. Therefore, students need *strategies* for determining word meaning (Nagy and Scott 2000). Students need to understand and know how to manipulate the structural

features of language. Most vocabulary-related school tasks naively presume this kind of knowledge. Classroom-based studies have demonstrated the effectiveness of two strategies that are particularly important for vocabulary development: teaching context clues and word parts (Baumann et al. 2005).

Context clues are frequently used as a reading strategy for determining the meaning of an unknown word. Although context in reading has many dimensions, it most often refers to figuring out the meaning of an unknown word by getting help (or clues) from the words, phrases, sentences, or illustrations surrounding it (Harris and Hodges 1995). The help that context provides may be semantic, i.e., based on the meaning of the surrounding words or sentences. It may also be structural, i.e., based on grammatical or syntactic markers within a word or a sentence.

Using context clues is an especially important strategy for vocabulary development because, as we noted earlier, many English words have multiple meanings. Since context is crucial in identifying which meaning to use, learning how to use the surrounding context helps students expand their vocabularies.

Morphological analysis, another important strategy, allows students to make connections among semantically related words or word families (Nagy and Scott 2000). By separating and analyzing the meaning of a prefix, a suffix, or another word root, students can often unlock the meaning of an unknown word. If we teach students that *bi* means "two," for example, they can use that information to figure out *biannual* or *biaxial*. When introducing the concept of "photosynthesis," we can point out its roots: *photo* means "light," *syn* means "with, together," and *thes* means "put." As students grapple with the complex process of how plants use "sunlight" (photo) to "put together" (synthesize) carbon dioxide and water to produce food, knowledge of these word roots will support their efforts.

Knowing that words can be broken into units of meaning is a powerful strategy for vocabulary development. Until recently, teaching word roots was a strategy reserved for upper-grade or content-area classrooms. But a growing body of research tells us that this strategy should be introduced early. In fact, by second grade, students should be adept at using word roots as a vocabulary strategy (Biemiller 2005). Learning key word parts will enable students to understand new words that are semantically connected. In this way, instruction becomes efficient—by learning one word part, students have clues to the meaning of all the words that contain it.

5. Vocabulary instruction must foster *word consciousness*, an awareness of and interest in words (Graves and Watts-Taffe 2002). Activities such as word exploration (e.g., word origins) and word play (e.g., puns and riddles) are central to vocabulary development. Moreover, they provide pleasant ways to accomplish the repetition necessary for students to learn new words.

Dictionaries and other reference works can add interest to a vocabulary program. Although most students begin to learn about reference tools in the primary grades, they may not know the enormous variety of apps and websites that are available. Some of them are really fun to use! (See Appendix A for some of our favorite reference sites.)

You can also share your own love of words. We all have favorite texts that we turn to because the words move us to laughter or tears. Reading these texts aloud to students and talking about the power of words is an effective practice. You can also whet students' appetites by sharing interesting word histories and then showing students how to explore the origins of words themselves. Posting lists of websites or print resources for students to investigate can help make word learning and word play priorities in the classroom as well. A vocabulary program should encourage students to become word sleuths, a habit that they may well carry with them throughout their school years and beyond.

Words themselves are just plain interesting, and our ultimate goal is to create lifelong word lovers. Digital games, crossword puzzles, word scrambles, riddles, and tongue twisters are fun, but they're also vocabulary practice. Make time for students to play and explore word games on their own or with others.

Vocabulary Development for English Learners

Students learning English as a new language have unique advantages as well as unique challenges. Their rich background experiences can be tapped to enhance learning for all students. English learners know how to move between two languages, integrating sounds and meanings into new words and grammatical structures. Their natural manipulation of two languages promotes higher-level thinking. Yet they sometimes feel lost in the unfamiliar linguistic and academic world in which they find themselves. And research has shown that learning English vocabulary is a crucial task for English learners (Nation 2001).

Becoming literate in a second language can take five to seven years, depending on the speaker's proficiency with their first language, the type of second-language instruction, and how much English the student knows at the time instruction begins (Pérez 2004). The beginning of this process can be worrisome for teachers: "Most new

English language learners will go through a silent period during which they are unable or unwilling to communicate orally in the new language" (Haynes 2007, 9). Yet at every stage of learning English, instruction can support students' learning.

Fortunately, everything we know about how to teach vocabulary applies to both first- and second-language learners: they need to focus on meaning by using research-based strategies to learn new words. They need frequent opportunities to try out new words in varied learning contexts. The major difference is that second-language learners generally require more distinctive scaffolding. There are two ideas that will help you plan vocabulary instruction for English learners:

- Use discussion to support word learning. Discussion opportunities benefit second-language learners by supporting their growth in conversational English as well as by promoting word learning. Students do not simply "soak up" language. They need *comprehensible input*—instruction slightly above their current language levels—that builds on prior knowledge. They also need lots of opportunities to practice, especially in small-group settings (Haynes 2007; Pérez 2004).

- Use students' native languages (or references to their native languages) whenever possible. Many English words have cognates in other languages. Spanish-speaking students can easily relate many new English words to Spanish because they share Latin derivatives. In teaching *aqueduct*, for example, students may already have the concept of "water" from the Spanish word *agua*. Encourage students to draw such connections between their first and second languages.

SUMMARY

We have presented a research-based rationale for addressing vocabulary in your classroom, five guiding principles to use when developing an instructional curriculum, and a few ideas about adaptations that may support your EL students. The following chapters and appendices elaborate on these ideas. We wish you success in your word journeys. In the end, we hope you and your students will agree with the British novelist Evelyn Waugh: "One forgets words as one forgets names. One's vocabulary needs constant fertilizing or it will die."

CHAPTER 2

A Root Awakening

In the first chapter, we discussed the importance of vocabulary in students' literacy development and academic success. We noted that as students advance through school, research indicates that they encounter increasingly more complex words and concepts (Blachowicz and Fisher 2015). Only those students who have mastered the conceptual, or content, vocabulary at a lower level are sufficiently equipped to unlock the meanings of academic words, particularly in the content areas.

It is clear, then, that knowing how to unlock the meanings of new words is an important lifelong skill for our students. Understanding how words work shows us how to think in new ways about words—those we already know and those that are new to us. In this chapter, we present some useful strategies and rationale for teaching vocabulary from a roots perspective. Then, we introduce the three kinds of roots. But first, what is a root?

What Is a Root?

Words, like stories, have structures. We all know that a good story has a beginning, a middle, and an end, and these parts connect with one another. Each part has a purpose and advances the overall story line. When we read and discuss stories with our students, we often ask, "What happens in this part of the story?" "What if this part of the story had been different?" "What happened before this part?" To understand a story, we often take it apart so we can think and talk about all the things that occur in the beginning, middle, and end of the plot. When our students create their own stories, we encourage them to think and compose in terms of these manageable and meaningful parts.

Likewise, many English words—and nearly all the academic words students must learn—are made up of parts. Like the parts of a story, the parts of a word also carry meaning. And this is precisely what a word root is: a part of a word that carries meaning. The technical name for a word root is a *morpheme*. Think about this for a moment before moving ahead. A word is composed of letters. But letters by themselves carry only sound, not meaning. The letter *r*, for example, has no meaning by itself. It's a sound, nothing more and nothing less. Letters, then, are word parts, but they are not roots because they have no meaning.

Similarly, the phonemes and word families, or *rimes*, that students learn to recognize in primary grades are associated with letters or letter combinations that produce sound but not meaning. Very young children learn to recognize the word family *–an* in such words as *fan, man, can, dandy, sand, dancer,* and *ran*. These words share a word family and two phonemes (/a/ and /n/), to be sure, but they have no shared meaning. Beginning readers need to develop fluency in recognizing letters and sound units because this enables them to say the words they see on a printed page. But a correctly decoded or pronounced word is understandable only when readers already know what it means. Thus, the skill of decoding does not generate growth in vocabulary or word comprehension. A student may know one hundred words with the rime *–an* and still be at a loss when encountering new words such as *phantom, sanitize,* and *tantrum*. The student may even be able to sound out these words, but the sounds generate no conceptual awareness. The sounds alone do not lead the student to the meaning of the new word; the student gets the sound but not the sense. However, teaching phonemes and word families *does* set the foundation for teaching students to look for word parts. Students learn that knowing a word part can lead to knowing other words.

Now, compare a word family with a word root. Remember how we defined *root*: a word part that carries meaning. A word root is a semantic unit; it means something. When a root appears inside a word, it lends its meaning to the word and thus helps create the word's meaning. Moreover, words that contain the same root also share

meaning. We call these related words *cognates* (from Latin *cognatus*, which means "born together, related in origin"). Notice how different this is from a word family, which only enables us to pronounce words. Like a word family, a root is also a group of letters. But unlike the word family, the root conveys sound *and* meaning.

Moving Along

One of the most commonly encountered roots in English words, for example, is *mot*. The root *mot* is not a word in itself, but it means something; it is a semantic unit. This particular root means "move." Nearly any time it appears in a word, that word will have a meaning associated with movement. Take a minute to think of *mot* words that have to do with movement—or better yet, ask students to do so! In a short time, even the youngest students can generate a list.

- A *motor* makes things move.

- A *motorcycle* moves down the street.

- A *locomotive* moves on tracks.

- Some outdoor lights are triggered by *motion* detectors.

- Some classrooms have a lot of *commotion*.

- We were *promoted* last year and moved ahead to the next grade.

- Who lost the *remote* control to the television?

By drawing a box around or otherwise highlighting the root that a group of words shares (*mot*), you can give your students a "root awakening." Words with a shared root have a shared meaning. They are cognates.

Why Teach Roots?

Many primary-grade students will be familiar with most, if not all, of the *mot* words in the above list. They are likely to have some awareness of *motors, motorcycles, locomotives, school promotions,* and—as any classroom teacher can attest to—*commotion.* These are familiar words and concepts, and by bringing them together in this way, students quickly come to understand the linguistic principle that words with the same roots are related in meaning.

Beyond this, teaching the meaning of a root such as *mot* equips students to build new *mot* words and expand their vocabularies. For example, you can write some of the following sentences on the board. Ask students to figure out the "movement" that can be found in their shared meanings.

- What *motivated* you to do that?

- What were your *motives* for saying this?

- What *emotions* did you feel when you learned the news?

- What is a *motif* in music?

- Do *promotion* gimmicks really work?

- Who wants to make a *motion* to end this meeting?

- My brother was *demoted* because of his unruly conduct.

With a roots approach to vocabulary learning, students discover how to look for meaningful connections between words they already know (such as *motor*) and words that they may not know (such as *motif*) as well as with words they may have heard before but only vaguely know (such as *demotion* or *motivate*). This discovery may also bring them a deeper understanding of a familiar word. Can you figure out the "movement" in *emotion*? When we teach vocabulary based on roots rather than word lists, we encourage our students to search for a word's meaning from the meaning of its root. By associating these words with their cognates, students become word sleuths as they ask questions about meaning and then try to answer them.

One way to help students think through and unlock the meaning of a word based on its root is to reword the sentence, substituting the root meaning for the word. For example: *What motivated you to do that?* can be translated as *What "moved" you to do that?* Another way is to define the word using the root meaning: a self-*motivated* student is a self-starter who "moves" on their own to learn. In fact, we often refer to someone with such energy as a "mover" and shaker. Similarly, our *motives* are the forces that "move" us to do or say certain things.

The possibilities are endless! Students will enjoy puzzling through some of the more challenging cognates. A *motif* in music is a theme or refrain that "moves" from part to part in the overall composition. When we hear a *motif* in one part of the symphony, we may hear it repeated in a different key in a later "movement." A *motif* in a novel is a theme that "moves" around the story, popping up here and there.

Applying root definitions also deepens students' understanding of a word's multiple meanings and introduces them to new usages. Students may know that being *promoted* means "advancing to the next grade" (*pro–* = "forward"). Asking students to consider other kinds of forward movement will get them to consider additional dimensions: a store needs to *move* its products *forward* in the market in order to sell more of them. Moreover, if a *promotion* is a "moving forward," then a *demotion* must be "moving downward" to a lower grade or a lower status. Even our *emotions* can be understood as feelings that "move" us. When we feel sad and cry, we might say we have been "moved" to tears. When our *emotions* are aroused, we might say we feel deeply "moved." And there is even movement when someone makes a *motion* in a business meeting. If the motion is seconded, the chairperson of the meeting then says, "It has been 'moved' and seconded that…"

Did You Know?

While students can learn only 8 to 10 new words per week through direct instruction, we know that there are dozens of words that come from the root *mot*. By learning just one root, students can easily add between 10 and 20 connected words to their vocabularies.

In Chapter 1, we mentioned that the same words can mean different things in different contexts. Confusion often results when a student learns a word as having one meaning, only to learn later that it can mean something else. A *promotion* to a higher grade in school is not the same thing as a sales *promotion*. But in either context, *promotion* retains its basic meaning of "the movement of something or someone ahead." This root-level awareness of words can be a real boon to our students. Let's consider the word *remote*. Most students will readily know what a *remote* control is. It allows us to change television channels without getting out of our chairs. We use a *remote* control when we are at a distance, or *removed* from, the TV. When the context changes and we later read or hear about a *remote* location, we can activate students' background knowledge by asking them to associate the known concept of "*remote* control" with the new concept of a "*remote* location." By talking about these two contexts that share the same word, we can guide our students to a root-level understanding. A *remote* control is far away from the TV, and a *remote* location is far away from most people.

In the previous chapter, we observed that students can learn only 8 to 10 new words per week through direct instruction. But we have just identified more than a dozen words that come from the root *mot*. By learning just one root, students can easily add between 10 and 20 connected words to their vocabularies.

Increasing Word Awareness

In Chapter 1, we talked about the need to build students' active and passive vocabularies. Most roots generate everyday words that students readily understand and actively use. However, the same roots also generate newer and harder content words

that will expand students' passive vocabularies. This is critically important to success in school because most school texts rely heavily on complex academic vocabulary that is not ordinarily used in daily conversation. When we teach roots, we reinforce the vocabulary that students have already acquired and then build on that reinforced foundation. The roots approach activates background knowledge and encourages students to advance from the known to the unknown.

Think back to our discussion of the root *mot*. Did you notice how easy it was to understand the root meaning of "move"? Roots have base-level meanings that are not conceptually difficult. They refer to essential things and actions that all language speakers understand. Since roots tend to have basic meanings, they enable us to understand even difficult words. Knowing what *movement* is, students can easily establish a connection between the movement of a motorcycle and the more sophisticated movement and motif of a symphony.

One final observation on the root *mot*. In Chapter 1, we noted that with continuing advances in technology, the English language will continue to add vocabulary of a scholarly, scientific, and technical nature. Think again of the phrase *remote control*, which came into existence only after the invention of electricity. The new device needed a name, and we created one from the appropriate root. In the computer age, we find the same root *mot* in a new form: the smiley face that showed up on-screen—cleverly called an *emoticon*. This new word was composed of word parts that carry meaning. An emoticon is an *icon* (image) viewed on a computer screen that indicates a particular *emotion*. As vocabulary is born to give names to new things and concepts yet to be created, Greek and Latin roots remain the foundation of our English language.

Roots are found in vocabulary from all phases of life. Seeing the world of words from a roots perspective fosters word awareness, the ultimate goal of all vocabulary instruction. It can be eye-opening for a third grader, for example, to connect a school word, such as *promotion*, to a mundane word, such as *motor*. Years later, the same student may be a part of the school band and quickly recognize a musical *motif* as coming from the same root as *promotion*. Like a motif in a lifelong symphony of learning, roots keep returning to us in new contexts. And roots, once learned, are rarely forgotten. Knowledge of roots will help your students throughout their lives engage in conceptual thinking about the fundamental meanings of words and the varieties of ways in which they can be used.

The Three Kinds of Roots

Roman military leader Julius Caesar famously wrote, "All Gaul is divided into three parts." Like a military general, we can employ the "divide and conquer" strategy (explained in

Chapter 4) to identify word parts that contribute to meaning. Many English words can be divided into three parts: the prefix, the base, and the suffix.

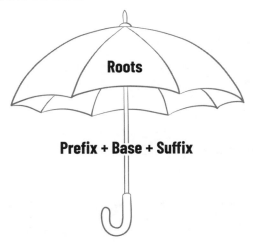

Roots

Prefix + Base + Suffix

Did You Know?

The concept of "divide and conquer" is a student-friendly term for word dissection. The strategy is used to identify semantic units and divide a word to unlock its meaning.

Prefixes, bases, and suffixes are the three kinds of roots, or semantic units, found in many words. Although sometimes the words *root* and *base* are used the same way, they are not interchangeable. *Root* is the generic term for any part of a word that holds meaning (Ayers 1986). Prefixes, bases, and suffixes are kinds of roots. In terms of a word's structure, the prefix appears at the beginning of a word, the base in the middle, and the suffix at the end. The umbrella diagram helps illustrate the distinctions between a prefix, a base, and a suffix.

Roots, then, is the umbrella term for the subcategories of prefix, base, and suffix. Notice that the *base* in the diagram is shown as the handle of the umbrella. The base holds up the entire word, providing its essential or "basic" meaning.

WHAT DOES A BASE DO?

As defined above, the base is the root that carries the basic meaning of a word. A base may be a word part (the base *duct* in *ductile, conduct, conduction*, etc.) or a stand-alone word (e.g., *duct*). Bases appear in everyday and academic words:

- *trac, tract* = pull, drag, draw
- *duc, duct* = lead
- *port* = carry
- *ven, vent* = come
- *sol, helio* = sun
- *dic, dict* = say, speak, tell

- *voc, vok* = call
- *viv, vit* = life
- *dom* = house

- *terr* = land, ground, earth
- *aqua, hydro* = water

These bases generate entire words that carry their basic meanings:

- A *convention* is a large meeting where people "come" together.
- A *motor* makes things "move."
- A *tractor* "pulls" farm equipment.
- A *duct* "leads" heated air from a furnace to the rooms of the house.
- A *porter* "carries" luggage.
- A *solarium* is a "sun" room. Earth follows a *heliocentric* orbit around the "sun."
- When students take *dictation*, they write exactly what the teacher "tells" them.
- A *vocation* is a profession that a person feels "called" to do (a "calling").
- Artwork created with *vivid* colors is considered bright and "lively."
- A *domicile* is a person's residence or "home."
- A *terrarium* is a glass enclosure for "earth" and soil to support plant and animal life.
- *Aquatic* animals live and thrive in "water."
- A *hydrofoil* operates in "water."

Notice that each of the italicized words in the above list has a meaning directly associated with the meaning of the base itself. In fact, the base *duct* can even function as a whole word all by itself! And as we noted earlier, these bases carry fundamental, easily understood meanings, such as "move," "pull," "say," "lead," and "carry." You may have noticed that none of the words in this particular list begins with a prefix. The first semantic unit in these words is the base itself.

WHAT DOES A PREFIX DO?

When a prefix is attached to the base of a word, the prefix does one of three things: gives a word direction, negates a word by meaning "not," or intensifies the meaning of a

word by adding the notion of "very." For this reason, we speak of three categories of prefixes:

- directional prefixes
- intensifying prefixes
- negative prefixes

Most of the prefixes found in English words—about 25 in all—are derived from Latin. Teaching the meaning of prefixes is especially helpful to young students because a few prefixes are used in a large number of words. In fact, nine prefixes account for 75 percent of the words that use prefixes (White, Sowell, and Yanagihara 1989).

Prefixes appear with such frequency in our vocabularies that students can easily learn some of them just by recalling words they already know. For example, a school has *exit* signs that point to the way "out of" the building. You can use this everyday word to teach that the prefix *ex–* sometimes means the direction "out, out of." *Ex–* can have an intensifying meaning as well. For example, an *exhausted* person is "very" drained (*haust* = "drain"). Another example of an intensifying prefix is the *per–* in *perfection*, which means "made very well, thoroughly done" (*fect* = "make, do"). Many students will have seen a band or an orchestra *conductor* wave a baton, leading musicians "together" as they play their instruments. You can use this familiar concept to teach that the prefix *con–* is a directional prefix meaning "with, together." When we tell students to *redo* an assignment, they know they must go "back" and do it "again." You can use this school experience to teach that *re–* is a directional prefix meaning "back, again." A person who is *unable* to come to a birthday party is "not" able to attend so: *un–* is a negative prefix. Likewise, *in–*, *im–*, and *il–* are negating prefixes. Consider words such as *invisible*, *impossible*, and *illegal*.

Most of the prefixes students encounter in school texts are directional in nature. This means that they indicate a path of some kind: "with, together," "under," "in," "out," "back, again," "away from," "down, off." Here are a few examples of the most common directional prefixes:

- *ad–* = to, toward, add to
- *e–*, *ex–* = out, out of
- *con–* = with, together
- *in–*, *im–* = in, on, onto
- *de–* = down, off
- *pro–* = ahead, forward, for
- *dis–* = apart, in different directions
- *sub–* = under, below

Once students have learned the directional meanings of these prefixes, they can generate a large number of words from even a single base. Here are some *trac, tract* ("pull, drag, draw") words with directional prefixes:

- Previews of coming *attractions* "draw" us "to" the theater.

- Muscles *contract* when they "pull" "together" and tighten.

- The ugly building *detracted* ("pulled" "down") from the beauty of the neighborhood.

- Noises in a school hallway are *distracting* because they "draw" our attention "apart" from the lesson.

- A dentist *extracts* a bad tooth by "pulling" it "out."

- A *protracted* war is one that is "drawn" "forward" in time and lengthened.

- When we *subtract* in a column of numbers, we "draw" the number that is "below" the higher one and take away from it.

All the italicized words above are cognates derived from a single base, *trac, tract*. Each of these words, furthermore, begins with a directional prefix that indicates the direction of the "pulling, drawing, or dragging."

WHAT DOES A SUFFIX DO?

If a word has a suffix, it comes at the end of the word. The essential function of a suffix is to indicate the part of speech of a particular word. We speak of noun suffixes, adjectival suffixes, adverbial suffixes, and verbal suffixes. We do not need to teach these grammatical concepts to young students, though. No one explicitly thinks about parts of speech when speaking or writing, and thankfully, it is not the purpose of vocabulary instruction to make students sound like dictionaries as they talk about a word and its range of meanings.

Suffixes, or word endings, rarely pose problems for students. The challenging portions of new words usually lie in either the prefix or the base. For example, it is unlikely that a student with grade-level English-language skills would refer to a *portable* television (*portable* is an adjective: "able to be" carried) as a *porter* television (*porter* is a noun: "one who" carries luggage). Once the student identifies the base of these words as meaning "carry," they are well equipped to deduce the meaning.

Although the ending of a word rarely poses a problem for students, a knowledge of suffixes greatly enhances their ability to become "flexible" with vocabulary words from the same base. For example,

- A *porter* carries luggage.

- A *portable* television can be carried from one room to another.

- A retailer engages in the *importation* and *exportation* of goods.

- We are *supportive* of one another.

In addition to increasing students' *flexibility* with words, suffixes are of great benefit in mastering words of Greek origin. Greek-based words tend to be long and often carry technical meanings. But by "dividing and conquering" the base from the suffix, students can quickly arrive at an understanding of the word's meaning. For example, consider words ending in *–ology* ("study of"):

- *Geology* is the "study of" the earth.

- *Hematology* is the "study of" blood.

- *Anthropology* is the "study of" human cultures.

SUMMARY

In this chapter, we have addressed some of the basics of word-root study. We have explained what we mean when we speak of roots, and we have offered some compelling reasons for root study as a way to build students' active and passive vocabularies. In a sense, a roots approach to vocabulary instruction induces (leads) students to think deeply about words and how word meanings are created. In the next two chapters, we will suggest some instructional basics. We will offer some strategies on how to "divide and conquer" words and how to "talk around" words in a way that will help students make connections between the new words they are learning and the old or current ones they already know. We will provide more sample roots—prefixes, bases, and suffixes—that teachers can use at various levels in elementary and middle school.

CHAPTER 3

Getting into Words:
Patterns, Sounds, and Meaning

Chapters 1 and 2 reviewed the research related to effective vocabulary instruction and introduced the notion of roots—word parts that carry meaning. The next several chapters expand upon these ideas by showing why and how to build a vocabulary program based on meaning-based roots. But first, consider an even more basic linguistic form—word families or rimes. This chapter, using examples from *Building Vocabulary: Foundations*, explains why and how early vocabulary and phonics instruction should focus on sound-based word families. And it all begins with patterns.

Why Patterns?

We live in a world of patterns. Simply look around and notice patterns that you may have taken for granted. Perhaps it is the shape of the stop sign or the configuration of

Did You Know?

Language patterns can take the form of stories, poems, or songs. The haiku, for example, is a very pattern-specific form of poetry. All haiku are defined by a structural pattern to which the writer must adhere.

colored lights on the stoplight at the end of your street. Maybe it is the consistent style of buildings in your neighborhood. Or perhaps it is the grid of streets in your city that makes navigating the streets and identifying specific locations easy.

Patterns are arrangements of repeated or corresponding parts—a recurring subject, theme, or idea; a distinctive and recurring form, shape, or figure. Detecting and using patterns makes life a bit easier. Knowing that a stop sign is a red octagon allows us to instantly recognize it and react appropriately. Imagine if stop signs were in all different shapes, sizes, and colors. It is likely that many drivers would misread them, and the result would be traffic chaos.

Human beings have the remarkable ability to detect patterns in their environments. Indeed, a research review by Mattson suggests that humans' superior pattern processing is the "fundamental basis of most, if not all, unique features of the human brain including intelligence, language, imagination, invention" (2014, 1). Mattson further points to language development as a particular form of pattern usage. He describes language as a "complex behavior in which auditory and/or visual patterns learned from other individuals or perceived in the environment are encoded, processed, and modified for the purpose of transfer of information to other individuals." Language patterns can take the form of stories, poems, or songs. The haiku, for example, is a very pattern-specific form of poetry. All haiku are defined by a structural pattern to which the writer must adhere.

Language patterns, however, can occur at the more molecular level. English sentences have a general pattern (noun phrase followed by verb phrase) that makes them easier for a listener or a reader who is familiar with this pattern to understand. Word placement also follows pattern rules: adjectives and noun markers usually precede the noun that they modify. And of course, written words themselves have patterns embedded within them that make both their decoding (symbol to sound) and their meanings easier to access.

Sound-Based Word Families

Cunningham (1998) notes that basic research on reading finds that the major word recognition function in the brain is pattern detection. The most beneficial sound-based pattern goes by a variety of names—word family, phonogram, vowel cluster, or rime. For the purposes of this book, we will use either the term *word family* or the more technical term *rime*. A word family or a rime in a written word is the part of a syllable that begins with the vowel and contains all letters within the syllable that follow. For example, in the word *bat*, the *–at* is the word family; in the word *bright*, *–ight* is the rime; and in *sound*,

–ound is the word family. The word *pattern* has two syllables, so it contains two rimes: *–at* and *–ern*.

The significance of sound-based word families is threefold. First and foremost, word families allow readers to be much more efficient decoders. Successful word decoding occurs when a reader recognizes a familiar spelling pattern in text and uses that knowledge of the pattern to decode a target word. As students become proficient with word families, they process the rime as a single unit, not as a collection of individual letters. For example, the word *bright* is not processed as six individual letters (*b-r-i-g-h-t*) but as two linguistic units: the consonant blend *br–* and the rime *–ight*. Imagine how much more difficult and inefficient it would be for a reader to have to examine and process words such as *bright* in a letter-by-letter fashion.

Second, rimes or word families represent reliable sounds. Although many phonics rules are riddled with exceptions, word families are quite consistent in their application. There are few, if any, exceptions to *–at* representing /at/ when *–at* represents a full syllable. Thus, we can be reasonably certain that when we teach students word families, we are providing a reliable and consistent phonics or sound representation of the word family.

The third benefit of word families is that they are ubiquitous—they are everywhere! Because every word in English consists of at least one syllable, every word contains at least one word family or rime. In a landmark study, Edward Fry (1998) attempted to identify the most important word families for students to learn as soon as possible. Fry reasoned that the first ones to teach are the ones with the greatest utility—the rimes that are found in the greatest number of words. His results are displayed below. According to Fry, knowledge of, and the ability to use, these 38 word families gives students the ability to decode and spell 654 one-syllable words! This is why word families are addressed throughout the *Building Vocabulary: Foundations* curriculum.

THE MOST COMMON WORD FAMILIES (RIMES)

–ab	–at	–ink	–ore	–unk
–ack	–ay	–ip	–ot	–y
–ag	–ell	–ight	–out	–ail
–est	–ill	–ow (how, chow)	–ain	–ew
–im	–ow (low, show)	–am	–ed	–in
–op	–an	–eed	–ine	–uck
–ank	–ick	–ob	–ug	–ap
–ing	–ock	–um		

And, of course, word families are found in multisyllabic words too. When we, as proficient readers, come to words we have not encountered before, we often decode the words not letter-by-letter but by examining them for word patterns (i.e., word families, bases, prefixes, and suffixes) that we have seen in our previous reading. For example, the word family –am can help students with words such as ham, Sam, jam, scram, slam, ram, and so on. But it can also help at least partially decode longer words, such as Alabama, hamster, camera, ambulance, examine, and quite literally thousands of others. Imagine the power we give to young readers when we enable them to take advantage of these word patterns.

How to Teach Word Families

A simple approach to teaching rimes or word families involves helping students develop an awareness and knowledge of target word families and then apply that knowledge in reading real texts and other activities. In this section, we explain several instructional routines using a lesson containing the word family –ock, which appears in Lesson 19 of the curriculum Building Vocabulary: Foundations, Level K. This model will give you a framework for thinking about how word-family instruction might look in your classroom. This instruction should last a couple of days. It's based on a simple poem that contains several –ock words.

Hickory Mickory Mock

Hickory mickory mock,
The mouse watched the clock tick-tock.
The mouse ran past
But not very fast.
Hickory mickory mock.

To begin, display the poem. Read it twice; point at the words as you read. Then, ask students to echo-read. (You read a line; they read the same line.) Finally, read the entire poem chorally with students. Continue this repeated reading when possible throughout the day. Also, have student pairs take turns reading the poem to each other.

The repeated reading of the poem helps students develop automatic recognition of not only the word family but also many whole words in the poem. Moreover, one of the great, and lesser-known, side benefits of reading poetry such as this is that it helps students develop another foundational reading competency—reading fluency. And the expression and rhythm needed to read the poem also develop prosodic oral reading skills, another critical reading competency.

Next, draw students' attention to the word family *–ock*. Write it on the board. Say it, and then ask students to say it with you. Next, reread the poem line by line. At the end of each line, ask students to say and spell the *–ock* words in that line.

Create a chart such as the one shown below. Add the *–ock* words from the poem. Write the words in a column so the letters from the word family are aligned. Ask students to spell the words for you. They can also write the words on whiteboards, on paper, or in their journals.

> **Word Family –o c k**
>
> m o c k
>
> c l o c k
>
> t o c k

The next day, read the poem to and then with students. Then, read the word chart to and then with them. Put *–ock* and these letters on the board: *s, r, cl, kn,* and *bl.* Play I'm Thinking of a Word. One at a time, ask the following questions, modeling the sound the letter or letters make as indicated by the slashes. Have student pairs answer the questions using *–ock* and one of the letters or blends on the board. Invite sharing. Put these new words on the word wall. Ask children to spell them as you write.

- I start with /s/. You wear me on your feet. You put me on before your shoes. What *–ock* word am I? (*socks*)

- I start with /r/. I can be found on the ground. If you throw me, I might break a window. What *–ock* word am I? (*rock*)

- I am how you tell time. I start with /cl/. What *–ock* word am I? (*clock*)

- I start with /kn/. I am what you do when a door is closed and you want someone to let you in. What *–ock* word am I? (*knock*)

- Students often build towers with these square toys. I start with /bl/. What *–ock* word am I? (*blocks*)

Practice reading the words on the word wall with students several times throughout the day—early in the morning, before lunch, after lunch, and before the end of the day. There are many strategies you can employ to keep instruction engaging:

- Read chorally as a group, starting from the bottom.

- Ask individual students to read the words.

- Shout the first word, whisper the second, etc., or read in silly voices (like a baby or a monster).

- Play games with the words (see Chapter 6).

- Send the words and poem home for students to read with their parents.

Over the course of the lesson, continually draw students' attention to the *–ock* word family. Be sure to talk about what the words on the list mean.

This basic lesson can be altered to offer differentiated support. Think about struggling readers, for example. You could use the poem to teach a variety of print-awareness concepts, rhyming, or letter recognition.

What do students learn during these brief instructional periods? These enjoyable activities give students opportunities to think about word family sounds and to review the many words containing the word families. Students build fluency in reading and build their sight vocabularies as well. Most importantly, they learn about how to use the sound-based word patterns to decode and spell successfully. We think this is a great use of instructional time!

Meaning-Based Word Patterns

Sound-based patterns are important, to be sure, especially for beginning readers. But perhaps more important as students move beyond the primary grades are meaning-based patterns, which are built upon morphemes. A *morpheme* is a language unit (sounds or letters) that carries meaning. Morphemes are particularly powerful for word learning in reading because the letters in morphemes not only represent sounds or phonemes, they also represent meaning. Morphemes can be individual letters, such as the *–s* at the end of words that means "more than one"; they can also be what we call bases, or whole words, such as *dog, car,* or *house*; they can be nonword bases that consistently carry meaning (e.g., *mot* = "move"); and they can be word segments that are affixed to the beginning or ending of words (e.g., *pre–* means "before," as in *preview*; *–ness* means "the state of," as in *heaviness*).

If we view word study as helping students detect and use patterns in words, then the next logical focus after sound patterns will be morphological patterns. And here we note that the most valuable morphemes to teach are those derived from Greek and Latin. The power of teaching Greek and Latin patterns or roots is that, much like sound-based patterns, the knowledge of one root can help students decode a multitude of English words. But unlike sound-based patterns, Greek and Latin roots can also help students determine the meaning of many words as well as their pronunciations. The remaining chapters in this book provide details about which morphological patterns (or roots) to teach and how to teach them.

The challenge in teaching Greek and Latin roots is that most teachers—most adults for that matter—are not very familiar with them. Surely, most of us know what the prefixes *pre–, re–, anti–,* and *sub–* mean. But these are only a very small fraction of all the roots that have found their way into English words. That is why one of the main purposes of this book is to provide you, the teacher, with awareness and background on these important patterns based on meaning so that you can bring them into play in your instruction, whether that is in English language arts or in the various content areas where academic vocabulary based on Greek and Latin roots flourish.

SUMMARY

The human brain has a unique ability to detect and use patterns. If we do not capitalize on this understanding in our phonics and vocabulary instruction, we are missing out on a great opportunity to expand students' word prowess—not only in terms of word decoding and spelling but also in terms of students' understanding of word meanings.

CHAPTER 4

A Developmental Look at Vocabulary Instruction

Lucas jumped into bed, eager for his dad to read him a bedtime story. It was one of his favorite times of the day. "We're learning all sorts of stuff about words in school," Lucas said as he got comfortable in his bed. Dad asked about what kinds of "stuff" he was learning, and Lucas told him about compound words. "Well, are you ready for your bedtime story?" Dad asked. Lucas replied with excitement, "Yep!" Dad showed Lucas the cover of a book of poems, including the picture and the title. "This book is called *Where the Sidewalk Ends*, by Shel Silverstein," Dad said. Then, they read the title together, pausing briefly after each word, when suddenly Lucas shouted, "Hey, *sidewalk* is a compound word, isn't it?"

Mr. Johnson, Lucas's first-grade teacher, had begun to teach students about the word families and roots we have described thus far in this book. To introduce the idea of roots, he began with the idea of compound words, since this is an easy way to help students understand that words can have *meaning chunks* as well as *sound chunks*. He used the instructional basics we outlined in Chapter 3, both the general principles to guide instruction and the routines that can constitute an effective vocabulary program. But he also thought about his students' developmental needs.

This chapter is about designing instruction that meets students' developmental needs. First, we focus on how to get students "into words." That is, how do we teach students *how* and *why* to look for meaning inside of words? How do we help students who are new to the classroom or new to the idea of root words?

Compound Words

As we mentioned in Chapter 2, we want primary-grade students to begin to think about roots (meaning units) as well as word families (sound or phoneme units). If this process begins with familiar words, students will develop this new understanding in the context of what they already know. In other words, we can get students into words by asking them to examine familiar words for parts that have meaning (their roots). The description below outlines procedures that have proven to be successful.

Begin with two-syllable compound words that students already know, as shown below. That is, students should know each word that makes the compound as well as the compound itself:

- bedroom
- football
- playground
- sidewalk
- birthday
- snowflake
- classroom
- doghouse

To introduce the idea of compounds, you might write a sentence on the board that includes one compound word:

*I painted my **bedroom** blue and white.*

Then, you can read the sentence to students while pointing to each word. Repeat a couple of times, if necessary, until you know that students know the words. At this point, you can draw students' attention to the compound word. Try posing a riddle: "What do you call the *room* where your *bed* is?" When students reply "bedroom," point to it in the sentence, and show students how *bedroom* is made up of *bed* and *room*. Try this a few more times:

Tomorrow is my **birthday**. What do you call the **day** of your **birth**?
Do you like to play **football**? What do you call a **ball** that you can kick with
your **foot**?

To conclude the lesson, tell students that *bedroom*, *birthday*, and *football* are called *compound words* and that compound words are made up of two words that, when put together, almost always tell the meaning of the compound word.

The next day, return to the examples. This time, simply read the sentences, and ask students to identify the compound word in each. As they do, remind them that compound words are made up of two words. Challenge students to identify the words. You might want to show the additive nature of compounds or compound words:

bed	+	room	=	bedroom
birth	+	day	=	birthday
foot	+	ball	=	football

You could also separate the words with a slash:

bed | room

birth | day

foot | ball

You may then want to offer more compounds. Ask students to divide each word into its two meaningful parts. Then, have them talk about each word, using phrases or sentences that include each of its units. They may offer statements such as "A *sidewalk* is something you *walk* along on the *side* the road"; "A *snowflake* is a *flake* of *snow*"; "The *playground* at our school has *ground* we can *play* on." The point is not to get technical about definitions. The purpose of the lesson is to get students thinking about how semantic units are connected to produce a new meaning.

After students understand the concept of compound words, invite them to be on the lookout for other compound words. They can hunt for other compound words on school posters, in advertisements, or in books from the classroom library. These words can be listed on a "Compound Words" word wall. Around the school, students might notice *hallway*, *desktop*, *whiteboard*, *notebook*, *backpack*, *laptop*, etc. If students offer suggestions that are two separate words rather than a compound word (e.g., *school clothes*, *high school*), accept their suggestions without belaboring the point that some words are written as two words. Remember, the overall goals are to build awareness and understanding of compound words and, more importantly, to support students' growing understanding that meaning can be found within word parts.

After students understand bisyllabic compound words, you can show them words that are three or four syllables long. Repeat the process just outlined, asking students to divide these slightly longer, but still easily recognizable, words into their component parts. Examples include *schoolteacher, storybook, dishwasher, mountaintop, countertop,* and *hairdresser.*

You can again ask students to generate words for the word wall, perhaps by asking them to think about their houses, special places, or favorite activities. They might come up with words such as *waterfall, loudspeaker, watercolors, scorekeeper,* and *honeybee.* Ask students to talk about each word using its component parts: "a *storybook* is a *book* with a *story* in it," "a *dishwasher* is a person or a machine that *washes dishes,*" and so on. By discussing easy, everyday words that are three syllables or longer, students begin to see that there is nothing intimidating about long words if they know how to "divide and conquer" them. Students could even be challenged to make their own compounds to describe themselves or their school (e.g., *smartgirl, superschool, tallguy*). The important thing at this early stage is to empower students to look inside words to find meaning, not just sounds.

Negating Words with Prefixes

After students have begun to understand that some word parts carry meaning, you can introduce the concept of prefixes (roots that appear at the beginning of a word). Prefixes can negate, suggest direction, or intensify. Begin with two common negative prefixes: *un–* and *in–*. Ask students to mark off the negative prefix, separating it from the rest of the word using a slash (e.g., *un/wrap*) or using an equation (e.g., *un + wrap = unwrap*). Then, ask them to identify the rest of the word. Invite them to talk about the word, this time using *no* or *not* in their descriptions. Start with words containing *un–* that present recognizable words when detached from the prefix. Examples include *unwrap, unable, unbutton, unhealthy, unzip, unclear,* and *unhappy.*

As students talk about these negated words, they may say, "After I *un*wrap my presents, they are *no* longer wrapped"; "My shirt is *not* buttoned if it is *unbuttoned*"; "When my jacket is *unzipped*, it is *not* zipped," and so on. This is an easy exercise, but it teaches an important skill: students are learning to translate a prefix into its meaning and combine the meaning of the prefix with the rest of the word.

We can then advance to the negative prefix *in–*, which also means "not."

- incorrect
- indefinite
- incomplete
- inhuman
- inaccurate
- invisible

The words are getting longer, but they can be divided, and their meanings can be deduced by working with the prefix. After students detach the negative prefix, they find that the rest of each word is fully recognizable. They simply translate these words as meaning "not correct," "not complete," "not accurate," and so on.

You can create riddles to support students' understanding: "What do we call something that is *not* visible?" You can also invite students to develop riddles for others to answer. Thinking about words in this way helps students see how to translate prefixes. Furthermore, they are getting used to the idea of "dividing and conquering"—and looking for meaning as they do so.

Some Directional Prefixes

Two directional prefixes lend themselves very well to instruction for primary-level students: *pre–* ("before") and *re–* ("back, again"). To introduce these to students, follow the same procedure recommended for compound words and the prefixes *in–* and *un–*. Present students with simple sentences that contain words beginning with these prefixes. After reading the sentences with students and identifying the target words, ask students to put a slash between the prefix and the rest of the word. Then, ask them to identify the intact word that remains. Everyday examples of *pre–* words include *presoak* laundry, *prewashed* lettuce, *preheat* an oven, *pregame* show, and *preshrunk* jeans.

Did You Know?

You can create riddles to support students' understanding: "What do we call someone who is *not* afraid?" You can also invite students to develop riddles for others to answer. Thinking about words in this way helps students see how to translate prefixes. Furthermore, they are getting used to the idea of "dividing and conquering" words—and looking for meaning as they do so.

After students remove the prefix, they are left with a word they already know. Ask them to talk about these words using the "before" meaning of the prefix *pre–* in their comments: "We *pre*soak heavily stained clothes *before* we wash them with other clothes"; "we *pre*heat the oven *before* we put the cookie sheets in"; "*pre*washed lettuce has been washed *before* we buy it at the store."

Do the same thing with the prefix *re–*. Again, use words that are recognizable after the prefix is detached. Ask students to talk about these words using "back" or "again" in their comments. For example, have them define *rewrite*, *rebuild*, *redo*, *reruns*, and *refills*.

Students may offer ideas such as: Go "back" and write this "again" (*rewrite*); I want you to go "back" and do your homework "again" (*redo*); This restaurant lets you fill your glass "again," and you can go "back" as many times as you want (*refill*); and so on.

This instruction may span several weeks. Take time to show students how words are made up of parts that have meaning. Give them ample time to practice in a lighthearted, fun way. Although the "divide and conquer" routine is presented with simple, familiar words, the concept itself is critical to further word learning. Students will be learning a strategy that they can apply to new words throughout their years in school and beyond.

Word Composition

So far, instruction has focused on recognizing words and word parts. We have presented compound words and words with prefixes and asked students to identify what they see. This helps students develop control over their passive vocabularies—the words they encounter when reading. Building active vocabulary is important too. A good way to approach this is to use riddles.

With the word wall visible, you might ask, "What do you do when you read a sentence 'again'?" They will answer, "We *reread* it." Ask, "When you are asked to make your bed 'again,' what do you do?" Answer, "We *remake* it." Answering these questions gives students practice in learning how to generate active vocabulary by producing the word that fits the context. This process—word composition—represents an important next step in students' word learning.

You might also ask students to generate silly words using the prefixes they have learned—a process most students enjoy. Student pairs can create riddles that describe a thing or an activity: "I am thinking of a word. What word is it?" Then, they can ask their classmates to produce the word they have in mind. They might make up words, which is perfectly acceptable for this activity. The goal is to enjoy word play.

*I wish I had "not drunk" all that milk. I wish I could **un**drink it.*

*I wish I had "not read" that story. If only I could **un**read it.*

*I spent all my money "before" I went shopping. I **pre**spent my money.*

*My mom drove me "back" to school because I had forgotten my books. She **re**drove me.*

What Are Students Learning?

Before we consider what is going on during these activities, we should ask what is *not* going on. Students are not learning word lists. They are not actively memorizing columns of individual words that have no relationship to one another. These surface approaches to word learning are not effective; students quickly forget words learned from memorized word lists. Nor is it efficient because, as noted in Chapter 1, research shows that students can learn only 8 to 10 new words per week through direct instruction.

For all their simplicity, the lessons we have described thus far in this chapter teach students several things at once. As they gain facility with the "divide and conquer" strategy, students find themselves thinking about roots, which appear over and over again not only in school words but also in their everyday speech. At the primary level, these word parts are often stand-alone words (e.g., *bedroom* and *snowflake*). Students learn to read the prefix *un–* as meaning "not," the prefix *pre–* as "before," and the prefix *re–* as "back, again." In the process, they apply these small semantic units over and over again to different bases, both in terms of taking words apart and putting words together. When they learn how to "divide and conquer," they also learn how to combine and create. Rather than memorizing word lists, the roots approach emphasizes learning the prefixes, bases, and suffixes that occur with the greatest frequency in the English language. Since there is nothing conceptually difficult about such words as *before*, *not*, and *again*, students can learn more than one root per week. Each root generates potentially dozens of words.

Did You Know?

The adage goes: "Give people fish and you feed them for a day; teach people to fish and you feed them for a lifetime." We can apply this wisdom to the teaching and learning of vocabulary. If we give students word lists, they may have vocabulary for the day. But if we teach them how to "divide and conquer" to determine word meanings, they will have vocabulary for life.

A well-known adage comes to mind here: "Give people fish and you feed them for a day; teach people to fish and you feed them for a lifetime." We can apply this wisdom to the teaching and learning of vocabulary. If we give students word lists, they may have vocabulary for the day. But if we teach them how to "divide and conquer" to determine word meanings, they will have vocabulary for life.

Some Easy Suffixes

Once students have grown accustomed to looking for prefixes at the beginning of words, they can learn to do the same thing with suffixes. By having students look at the beginning and end of a word, they learn to search for word parts that have meaning: the word's beginning, middle, and end. Take examples from what students already know to draw their attention to suffixes. Teach a few suffixes that have fixed meanings. Our goal is not to teach them all the suffixes, only to draw their attention to them and teach students how to work with suffixes. Below are some useful and easy suffixes:

- *–able*, *–ible* = "can, able to"
- *–er* = "more"
- *–est* = "most"
- *–ful* = "full of"
- *–less* = "without, lacking"

You can present the suffixes *–er* and *–est* in a single lesson, and sequence adjectives such as *small, smaller, smallest; tall, taller, tallest;* and *smart, smarter, smartest.* The base of each of these words is already known: *small, tall,* and *smart.* Explain that when we add the suffixes *–er* and *–est* to words such as these, we change the meaning of the base word. (These are adjectives, but it is not necessary to get into the technicalities of parts of speech at this stage.) Students can draw pictures of three things of varying sizes. One student may draw three dogs: one is small, another is "more small," and the third is the "most small." The student may caption each drawing with "small dog," "smaller dog," "smallest dog." Another student may draw three houses or three people. Students can create additional drawings without labels and ask another student questions such as, "Which is the smallest house?" "Which is the smaller of these two houses?"

By looking at these suffixes as units with meaning, students quickly learn that they can change the meaning of a word by adding a suffix to a base word, by removing a suffix, or by changing the suffix. In the process, they learn that since a word is made of parts that have meaning, they can figure out the meanings of words by looking for parts. These parts appear over and over again in words they encounter every day.

Likewise, we can teach the two suffixes *–ful* and *–less* as a set and have students generate antonyms:

careful	careless
colorful	colorless
harmful	harmless
hopeful	hopeless
meaningful	meaningless
painful	painless
powerful	powerless
thoughtful	thoughtless
useful	useless

You might begin by showing students two pictures—one in color and the other in black and white. Ask, "Which one is *colorful?*" and "Which one is *colorless?*" You could also show *careful* and *careless* children, *painful* and *painless* facial expressions, and so on. Then, you might ask students to make quick sketches. Have students sketch something *useful* and something *useless.* Finally, students can draw pairs of pictures and caption them with words of opposite meaning: a *careful* student as opposed to a *careless* student, a *colorful* shirt as opposed to a *colorless* shirt. These activities help students learn that the same base can produce words of opposite meaning depending on the suffix.

Invite students to engage in word play. They can create their own words by using a single suffix. The suffix –*able* lends itself well to this exercise. As students attach this suffix to any number of existing words, they can talk about the meanings they have generated:

- A *readable* book: it "can" be read.

- A *doable* assignment: it "can" be done.

- A *washable* jacket: it "can" be washed.

- An *unthinkable* idea: it "cannot" be thought.

Silly examples can be fun as well:

- My dog is *unwalkable* because he refuses to wear a collar and leash: he "cannot" be walked.

- My jacket is *unzippable* because it only has buttons: it "cannot" be zipped.

- My bed is *unsleepable* because the mattress is so lumpy: it "cannot" be slept in.

All these activities help students make the cognitive leap that words contain much more than letters and sounds; many are also made up of semantic units—roots. Just as the roots of a tree are essential to the tree's life, the roots of a word are essential to the word's meaning. They may not have noticed roots before, but "dividing and conquering" a word makes them visible. Word awareness is beginning! Students are uncovering what is inside a word as they dig for its roots.

These activities also embolden students to think as they speak and write. They learn that word mastery involves two skills. As lifelong readers and listeners of words, they will always be encountering vocabulary they can "divide and conquer." Furthermore, as lifelong speakers and writers, they will benefit from combining and creating roots as they come up with the right words for the right context. But perhaps most importantly, when we ask students to generate vocabulary by using prefixes and suffixes, we are preparing them for the most important part of the "divide and conquer" strategy: zeroing in on the base.

Back to "Basics"

Most likely, when you help students learn to focus on prefixes and suffixes, they will notice that prefixes and suffixes always attach to something else in the word. That "something else" is the base. Of the three kinds of roots (prefix, base, suffix), the base is the most important. Indeed, the base is the crucial part of the word: it provides the word with its essential, core, or "basic" meaning. That meaning is affected by the prefix and by the suffix. By themselves, a prefix or a suffix cannot generate a word. There must always be a base.

Fortunately, the meanings of bases derived from Greek and Latin are usually straightforward. Our sample base in Chapter 2 was *mot* meaning "move." Consider the meaning of these two Latin bases:

- *audi, audit* = "hear, listen"
- *vid, vis* = "see"

The meaning of many words built on such bases is often immediately clear. An *audible* sound, for example, is one that "can" be "heard." A *visible* image "can" be "seen." An *inaudible* voice "cannot" be "heard," just as an *invisible* force "cannot" be "seen." An *auditorium* is a large room for "listening" to speakers or performers. The *audio* portion of a TV program is the part we "hear" (as opposed to the *video* portion, which we "see"). When we *audition* for a school play, we must speak a part, sing a song, or play an instrument for the judges to "hear" or "listen" to. A *vista* offers a panoramic view and enables us to "see" large expanses of scenery. We wear sun *visors* to shade our eyes so that we can "see" things in the glaring sunlight. In words such as these, the straightforward meaning of the base leads directly to the meaning of the entire word. Students will quickly find the basic idea of "hearing" or "seeing" as readily *evident* in these words (*e–* = intensifying prefix; things that are *evident* are "very" easy to "see").

"Metaphors Be with You": Helping Students with Figurative Meaning

Words that are metaphorical in meaning are some of the most challenging for students, as they have figurative or implied meanings rather than straightforward or literal meanings. How are we to help students understand that words such as *advise* and *provide* are also derived from *vid, vis*? The basic and literal meaning of "see" isn't readily evident in these words. But if you begin an exploration of *vid, vis* with words related to actual physical "seeing," you can scaffold students' learning about this other, more abstract "seeing." To do this, you can return to the overall procedure we described earlier—ask students to talk about (i.e., not define) the words and figure out how they contain the basic idea of "seeing" on perhaps a different level from that of physical eyesight.

Let us consider the word *supervisor*, and talk about it in terms of "seeing" (prefix *super–* = "over"). A supervisor is someone who "oversees" someone else's work. Ask students to talk about supervisors and what they do. We may speak of a supervisor at work as hovering over us and watching our every move. The basic meaning of "seeing" forms the core of this word. A supervisor takes a close "look" at another's work and inspects it for accuracy. We might ask, for example, "What does a *supervisor* do? What could this have to do with 'seeing'?" As students offer ideas, rephrase their answers to focus on the words *seeing, watching,* or *looking*. This will help students begin to think about "seeing" both literally and figuratively.

We can find the same basic idea of "seeing" in the words *provide* and *provisions*. We use these words in such contexts as "providing for our children," "providing for a rainy day," and "buying weekly provisions at the grocery store." When we shop for our *provisions*, we are "seeing" "ahead" (*pro–* = "forward, ahead") to what we will need for the coming week. When we *provide* for our children, we are "seeing" "ahead" to their future needs. We are *envisioning* the future, trying to form a mental picture of what they will need. The basic sense of "seeing" in all these words is not literal but figurative.

But how are we to teach the concept of figurative uses of language in vocabulary lessons? Isn't this something we find in poetry and other high forms of literature? Actually, figurative language abounds in our daily speaking. We use the word *see* on a literal and figurative level, and we use these two levels without even thinking about the difference. As linguists George Lakoff and Mark Johnson (1980) have demonstrated, figurative language, especially metaphors, guide our very thought processes. They are embedded in our vocabulary because they are embedded in our thinking. As we discuss the word *supervisor*, we can invite students to recall phrases from our daily speech when we might say "see" without referring to physical eyesight. We might say, "Don't you *see* my point?" In this context, *see* refers to understanding, to "seeing" something with the mind's eye, as it were. This meaning of *see* in "Don't you *see*?" is different from saying, "Don't you *see* that bus?" When we *see* a bus, we literally *see* it with our eyes. When we *see* someone's point, we take the basic meaning of "see" and apply it to other contexts—even with our eyes closed! When something is *evident*, we say, "Oh, now I *see*!"

Did You Know?

The base *vid*, *vis* can be found in the words *provide* and *provisions*. These words are used in such contexts as "providing for our children" and "buying weekly provisions at the grocery store." When we shop for our *provisions*, we are "seeing" "ahead" (*pro–* = "forward, ahead") to what we will need in the future. When we *provide* for our children, we are "seeing" "ahead" to their future needs. We are *envisioning* the future, trying to form a mental picture of what they will need. The base meaning of "seeing" in all these words is not literal but figurative.

You can help students see the differences between these two kinds of "seeing" by presenting phrases or sentences containing *see*:

- Do you *see* my point?
- Do you *see* the rainbow?
- *See* to it.
- *See* the pretty picture.
- Now I *see* what you mean.
- Now I *see* a storm cloud.

Ask student pairs to sort these into two categories: physical seeing and figurative seeing, or "seeing with our eyes" and "seeing with our mind's eye." When sharing their work with the rest of the group, be sure to invite their thinking about which kind of *seeing* is being referred to in the phrase or the sentence. You could even post two charts in the classroom and ask students to add examples they encounter.

On the one hand, understanding the meaning of bases on a figurative level poses a challenge to teachers and students. On the other hand, these bases provide a fascinating entrance into the world of conceptual and abstract thinking. Our everyday speech is filled with figurative language. It abounds in colloquial, or everyday, English, and these colloquialisms can often lead us to an understanding of words' meanings.

Polysemy: Helping Students Understand Multiple Meanings

Learning to think about words' figurative meanings can help students with another common challenge. In Chapter 1, we mentioned that a word such as *revolution* means one thing in science class (e.g., the revolution of Earth around the sun) and another thing in social studies (e.g., the American Revolution). This polysemy can pose a problem for students, but knowing roots and how to think figuratively about meaning can lead to solutions. We can advise students to examine the context of a polysemous word to figure out what it means *this time*. Guiding students to contextual clues remains an important part of vocabulary instruction, but the roots approach offers additional support. If students know that the base of the word *revolution* is *volut*, meaning "roll, turn," they can work with the base meaning and arrive at a correct understanding of the word in each context. In science class, we speak literally of Earth "rolling, turning" around the sun as it physically moves through space. But in social studies, we speak of revolution figuratively, in terms of the first Americans "overturning" British rule of the colonies. Revolutions upset things because they "turn" political situations upside down. The basic idea of "rolling, turning" lies at the core of the word *revolution* whether we are speaking of the American Revolution or the revolution of the moon around Earth. To drive the meaning of the base home, we might tell students that the first books (which we now call *volumes*) were made of "rolls" of ancient paper called papyrus!

"Run" with This

Let's think about the literal and figurative meanings of bases with another example. The Latin base *cur(r)*, *curs*, *cour(s)* means "run." In many words, this base refers to physical "running" or something close to it: a *courier* service "runs" letters and packages with runners who either run on foot, ride bikes, or drive delivery trucks. The idea of "running, speed, and rapid movement" is evident in this word. We may also think of a *racecourse* on which athletes, cars, or horses physically "run."

What about writing in *cursive* script? There is no physical running in writing cursive. In fact, we usually write cursive from a seated position! In this word, the "running" occurs on a figurative level. In cursive, the letters "run" together with ligatures, and we can write more quickly than by printing letters. As we think about figurative running, we observe that the *cursor* on our computer screen "runs" across the monitor as we move the mouse. The *current* of a river has "running water." Reflect on this phrase for a moment. If we thought about in merely literal terms, the phrase "running water" might sound absurd. Water does not run—it flows, it spills, it drips—but it does not literally run. It figuratively runs. The figurative meaning also pertains when we speak of *current* events or of films *currently* showing at the theater. These events and films are now "running," so to speak. We employ figurative language in our daily speech, and this can lead us to a roots-level understanding of many words.

Here are a few more "running" words that employ figurative language. We speak of cash as *currency* because money is viewed as flowing, fleeting, "running"—similar to the *current* of water. Compare phrases such as "cash flow," "liquidated assets," and "frozen assets." We *incur* debts and "run up" our bills. When we *concur* with others on an issue, we agree with them because our ideas "run together with" theirs. When we take an *excursion*, we are usually "riding out," rather than "running out." Nevertheless, the basic figurative use of "running" applies. Likewise, one country may conduct a military *incursion* of another—an aggressive "running into" someone else's territory. The invading soldiers may arrive in tanks or by parachute without actually running on foot. In a relatively new application of the word *incursion*, we hear of *runway incursions* at airports with heavy traffic. Airplanes have near misses and almost "run into" one another as they land and take off.

After students develop some proficiency with identifying bases in words, spend time challenging them to think about both literal and figurative meanings in words with the same base. Display several words with the same base in phrases or sentences, and ask student pairs to talk about how the word reflects the meaning of the base. Then, invite whole-group sharing. As you can, remind students that many words with bases have multiple meanings (e.g., *courses* in school, race*course*, the *course* of events). These activities help students learn to think flexibly about what words mean and how they work.

A Coherent Pedagogy

As we focus on word roots with their literal and figurative meanings as well as common words with multiple meanings, we get students talking about their school vocabulary in everyday speech. This is important for several reasons.

First, it removes a potential fear factor from vocabulary. Dictionary definitions can be intimidating for students. They often look up a new word only to find that the definition is just as hard to decipher as the word itself. Formal definitions that include phrases such as *characterized by*, *pertaining to*, and *having a tendency to* do not have a particularly inviting tone that will encourage students to keep reading. This feature can intimidate students into not wanting to open a dictionary or search online for definitions! If students think that they have to sound like a dictionary in order to know a word, they may quickly become discouraged and give up, saying, "I can never talk like this. No one talks like this!"

Second, students learn that by thinking about a word in terms of its roots, they often have background knowledge they can activate. They simply may not have realized that they had this foundation already at their disposal. Students may never have heard a word such as *incursion* before, but they all know what *run* means. By approaching vocabulary on this literally "basic" level, students learn to simplify something that they initially find complex. *Incursion* is a difficult word when first encountered, but the concepts of an army "running into" enemy territory (*military incursion*) or of one airplane "running into" another (*runway incursion*) are understandable.

Third, as students focus on the roots they recognize inside a new word, they can become inspired to recall words they already know but perhaps never thought about as cognates. Students thus learn that words have their own families and that words with the same base all share a basic meaning. A student who first encounters a word like *incursion* and identifies the base as meaning "run" may well associate it with words they either use or hear all the time—words such as *current, currency, course, cursor,* and *excursion.* These moments of discovery when a student sees a connection between a new word and one or more cognates can be exciting. The student is not only learning a new word but also linking it to knowledge already acquired.

Finally, the roots approach to vocabulary teaching and learning mirrors the very process through which we, as users of language, arrive at an understanding of new ideas and concepts. Let's take the example of the *automobile.* We all know what automobiles are, of course, but this was not always the case. When the automobile was first invented, we had no word to describe this strange machine on wheels that was able to move itself without an animal to pull it. So we gave it a name from two roots: the Greek *auto–,* meaning "self," and the Latin *mobil,* meaning "move." The Greek and Latin roots in the newly contrived word gave us a handle on understanding the novel invention. But this contraption was so novel that we could not fully understand it without likening it to something we already knew. We could only understand the word *automobile* by activating our background knowledge. So we turned to the horse and buggy, the only device that offered something comparable; this was our figure or metaphor for conceiving of this contraption. We thus arrived at a clear understanding of the automobile through metaphorical or figurative thinking.

We still see signs of this pattern of thought in words and phrases such as the "horsepower" of an engine; the "power train" (think of "wagon train"); and the very words "car" (from the original "horseless carriage"), "drive" (originally, to get a horse or cattle moving), and the "ride" of a car. We still speak of cars "breaking down"—a phrase first applied to horses whose strength gave out—and of riding "shotgun" in the front seat (originally, the position for the gunman on a horse-drawn wagon, beside the driver). To this day, automobile marketers invoke our figurative thinking with such names for their products as Bronco and Mustang.

The point here is simple but very important: as thinkers and users of language, we all come to understand new things only in terms of what we already know (schema). This is how reading comprehension, indeed all learning and its associated vocabulary, occurs. We activate our own background knowledge by likening the new concept or invention to something familiar. In the process, we approach the new idea on a "basic" level to which we then apply both literal (e.g., a *courier* physically "runs" to deliver packages) and figurative (the *cursor* figuratively "runs" across my computer screen) understandings. The roots approach to vocabulary mirrors this very process. Thus, as we teach our students to "get into words" at the root level, we actually invoke the same thought processes all users of language invoke when they advance from the known to the unknown. This pedagogy is in line with the very evolution of our language and our own development as language speakers. As Wexler (2019) makes clear, it is impossible to equip students with all the vocabulary they need by teaching it to them directly. Instead, we need to give them the tools to think about how words work—unlocking student potential for understanding vocabulary.

SUMMARY

In this chapter, we described a developmental sequence for teaching students about units of meaning in the words they encounter. We begin with compound words because they are concrete, familiar, and useful for making the "meaning" point. If you teach at the primary level, spend a few weeks on compounds. The common prefixes and suffixes presented in this chapter are also an appropriate instructional emphasis for young students. You may need less instructional time with older students who are beginning roots study. The time you spend—whether several weeks or a few days—is important, for it helps students understand the core of this approach: many words are made up of meaning units.

The figurative meanings of common bases also deserve instructional attention, even with primary-grade students. Once students become accustomed to this way of thinking about words, it is amazing how easily they embrace it. Asking what the American Revolution has to do with the base *volut* ("turn"), for example, poses an interesting challenge. It invites critical thinking about the word and also the concepts represented by the word.

The *Building Vocabulary from Word Roots* curriculum provides rich and ample discussions of the literal and figurative meanings of all the bases presented, as well as more examples of compounds, prefixes, and suffixes. Roots-based vocabulary instruction turns even young children like Lucas, who was mentioned at the beginning of the chapter, into word sleuths.

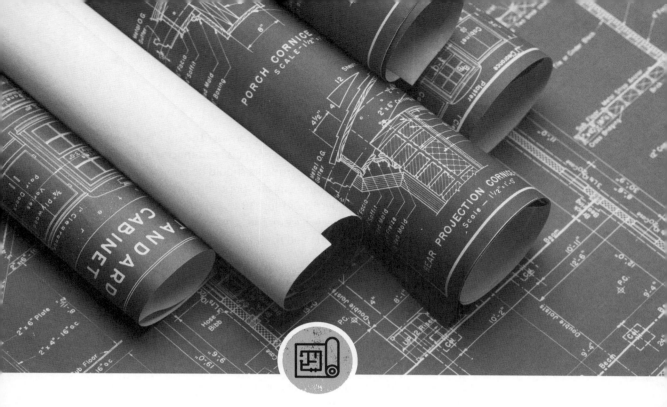

CHAPTER 5

Planning Vocabulary Instruction & Assessment

In the first chapters of this book, we built a research-based rationale for the importance of vocabulary instruction. We also explained our focus on word parts (or roots) and offered suggestions about which word parts to use as the basis for instruction. In this chapter, we draw upon all this background information and focus on ideas for planning vocabulary instruction. First, we address instructional basics like time and how to develop an instructional model. Next, we explain several instructional routines; we show them in action using a sample week from the *Building Vocabulary from Word Roots* Level 5 curriculum (Rasinski et al. 2019). Finally, we offer some advice about differentiating instruction and assessing students' vocabulary growth.

Instructional Planning: The Basics

Before developing an instructional model, you should consider the issue of time. How much time per day can you devote to vocabulary instruction? Daily attention to vocabulary is important, because as we noted in Chapter 1, students should be immersed in words with frequent opportunities to use them in diverse oral and print contexts in order to learn them on a deep level (Lehr, Osborn, and Hiebert 2004). Just 10 to 15 minutes focused on vocabulary instruction and guided practice each day will foster this sense of immersion. For your vocabulary program to meet its goals, you need to devote consistent time to it.

We think there are three important points to consider when deciding on an overall instructional model.

1. First, you need a routine. Although incidental word learning is important and powerful (NRP 2000), it is not enough. Certainly, occasional "teachable moments" enrich word study. But this hit-or-miss way of working with words cannot, by itself, lead to the deep word learning we seek.

   Consider, instead, developing an instructional routine—a consistent block of time that features a predictable set of learning opportunities and activities. This allows you to maximize instructional time and minimize time spent giving directions or explaining procedures (Rasinski, Padak, and Fawcett 2010). Students will know what is coming and how to participate effectively. For example, if "divide and conquer" is one of your routines, you won't have to waste instructional time explaining its procedures each time you do it. Instead, students will know how to think about the general instructional protocol and can devote their attention to the particular word elements for that lesson.

   Routines do not have to be routine. We hope that reading aloud to your students is one of your daily routines. Because you read something new each day, your read-aloud is not routine—it is predictable. Students look forward to it and know how to act and respond during a read-aloud. So it is with vocabulary routines. Students know that they will spend time each day thinking about and learning new words. This sends a subtle message about what's important in your classroom—words and vocabulary.

2. A second point to consider in developing an overall instructional model can be summarized in two words: teachers teach. Making assignments, monitoring students' activity, and assessing students' work are surely part of your day, but they are not *teaching*. Showing, modeling, telling, scaffolding, explaining—these teaching actions will enhance your students' vocabulary learning.

3. A third point to consider is that you base instructional routines on a gradual release of responsibility (Weaver 2002). At the beginning, when students need

the most support, you might lead the discussion and model how an activity is done. Later, as students develop some control over the new learning, small groups or student pairs working under your guidance can offer the scaffolding students need. Eventually, the goal is for students to "show what they know" independently. So your goal should be an overall approach that begins with teacher-led instruction followed by activities that scaffold increasingly independent learning.

Recommendations for Instructional Routines

Here are a few recommendations for your instruction. Spend about 10 to 15 minutes each day on vocabulary; make sure the instruction focuses on selected word parts or roots; and gradually release responsibility to students. With these general ideas as a framework, we now describe several routines that collectively will enable you to achieve your goals for students' word learning. Note that instructional routines for young students (those in kindergarten through grade 2) are outlined in Chapter 3. You'll see similarities between those recommendations and the ones we make below. The chief difference is that younger students work with word families and older students focus on roots that carry meaning.

We recommend that you begin each week (or instructional cycle of your choosing) by inviting students to "meet a root or word family." If you are using the *Building Vocabulary* curriculum, these selections have been made for you. The next stage in instructional planning is to develop routines based on this root. There are five routines at the core of the *Building Vocabulary from Word Roots* curriculum that give students practice working with a root in a variety of ways that require different kinds of thinking: Word Spokes, Divide and Conquer, Read and Reason, Combine and Create, and Extend and Explore. On the following pages, each routine is explained with reference to instruction that focuses on *struct*, which means "build" (Level 5, Lesson 15 of the *Building Vocabulary from Word Roots* curriculum).

MEET THE ROOT: WORD SPOKES

Begin instruction by sharing the root and its definition with students. Then, provide a few familiar words containing the root. Ask students to turn and talk: "Where is the meaning of the root in these words?" For example, you could present questions that include the root *struct*:

What does a **construction** worker do?

Why is the period after the Civil War called **Reconstruction**?

After student pairs talk, invite whole-group conversation, stressing the meaning of the root as much as possible. Next, display Word Spokes. The example shows the root at the center with a few words built from it in the outer spokes.

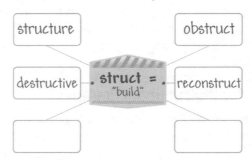

Have student pairs complete the activity by discussing how each word on the spoke reflects the meaning of the root. Then, add new words containing the root to the graphic, and write sentences containing the new words. Whole-group discussion follows each step, always underscoring root meaning.

To conclude the activity, begin a word wall (or classroom display) with students. Include the words discussed thus far, and encourage students to add others they encounter throughout the week. Use these words for a variety of practice activities, such as challenging students to use them in conversation and writing or sorting words in a variety of ways (e.g., by number of syllables, presence or absence of prefixes or suffixes). Find simple and informal ways to draw attention to the words on the word wall throughout the day and week.

DIVIDE AND CONQUER

We believe that the strategy of "divide and conquer" (word dissection) is the single most powerful vocabulary activity. It helps students see the root in the context of words so that they can learn how to identify it and use its meaning to determine the meaning of unfamiliar words. With "divide and conquer," students "dissect" words by looking for familiar prefixes, suffixes, and a common base. A short list of cognate words (i.e., words that share a common base) provides a good introduction to this activity. You might start with a list of words like these that are all built on the Latin base *struct*, which means "build":

- structure
- construct
- construction
- obstruct
- deconstruct
- infrastructure
- reconstruct
- superstructure

Begin by activating background knowledge and drawing students' awareness to the everyday occurrence of this root in their existing vocabularies. Most students will know that a *structure* is a building. Many have had to drive through *construction* zones, in which they saw things being built along the roadside.

You can also activate background knowledge by focusing on the prefixes found in some or all of these words, depending on those that students know. You can ask them to talk about these words and use the meaning of the base (they should say "build" in their responses) and the meaning of the prefix (*con–* = "with, together"; *de–* = "down, off"; *re–* = "back, again"). They may come up with the following suggestions: When we *construct* things, we put a lot of different parts (bricks, cement, wood) "together" and "build" them. When they *deconstruct* a building, they knock the "building" "down." When we *reconstruct* something, we "build" it "again."

After students have thought about the literal "building" in *struct* words such as *construction* and *reconstruction*, you can ask them to consider more figurative words meaning "build." For example, provide familiar words such as *instruct*, *instructor*, and *instruction*, and ask students what these words have to do with "building." Students will know that these words all deal with *teaching*: a teacher is an *instructor*, and all students are asked to follow *instructions*. You can guide students in a brief discussion around what school and teaching are all about: Our *instructors* "build" us up by teaching us things we need to know. They "build" our knowledge. In what ways is a teacher like a "builder"? A teacher lays a strong foundation for learning—just like a "builder" who lays a foundation for a building. A little discussion gets the class to think about the general idea of "building" in figurative as well as literal terms.

Did You Know?

The *Building Vocabulary* curriculum includes Digital Games for students to practice the skills of "divide and conquer" and "combine and create."

Scan the QR code, or visit tcmpub.com/bv-games and click "How to Play" for a quick tutorial!

This activity takes only a few minutes and serves an important purpose: students focus their attention on the new root by connecting to familiar words. You help them do this by scaffolding the conversation through examples, tasks, and questions. After the conversations described above, for example, students can independently "divide and conquer" *struct* words, beginning with single-prefix or single-base words, such as *infrastructure*, and moving to more complex words, such as *reconstruct* and *indestructible*.

READ AND REASON

Learning how to use the surrounding context—whether grammatical, structural, or oral—helps students expand their vocabularies. Using context clues is an especially important strategy for vocabulary development because, as we noted earlier, many English words have multiple meanings. Identifying which meaning is the best fit depends entirely on context. Moreover, the reason we learn new words is to use them in authentic language experiences—to understand them in our reading and listening and draw upon them for our writing and speaking. The "read and reason" activity offers students these opportunities. Students read extended texts—journal entries, advice columns, news accounts, poetry, stories, dialogues, and so forth. These contain several words that feature the root that is the focus of instruction. After reading, students answer questions that depend upon knowledge of both the text they have read and the root they have been studying.

The "read and reason" activity below is about the study of the *struct* root, meaning "build." After reading, students answer questions about road construction and how to "divide and conquer" the word *infrastructure*.

Read and Reason

Directions: Read the passage. Pay attention to the italicized words. Then, answer the questions.

Have you ever driven on a highway in the United States? The interstate highways that span our country are getting old. Each spring, *construction* work begins on our highways, especially on bridges and overpasses. Many of these *structures* have grown weak over time from the constant vibrations of passing cars and trucks.

Weather has also taken a toll on our roads. Each year, it is necessary for us to *reconstruct* some bridges and rebuild many roads. You can always spot repair sites because *construction* workers use flags to direct traffic around orange barrels and cones that line the work areas. Drivers must slow down in these *construction* zones. Sometimes, their equipment *obstructs* traffic and causes delays.

We call our system of highways and bridges an *infrastructure*. The Latin prefix *infra–* means "beneath, below." All roads and bridges are installed deep beneath ground level. This makes them *structurally* secure. But this is also why *reconstruction* projects take so long. Repairs are difficult because changes must be made "from the bottom up." If you pay attention to news broadcasts and articles in newspapers, you are bound to run into the word *infrastructure*.

1. What do you think is the most interesting information in this passage? Explain why.

2. What does *structurally secure* mean?

3. What italicized word in the above text refers to a traffic jam?

4. The word *infrastructure* is made up of two Latin roots. What are they, and what do they mean?

COMBINE AND CREATE

Knowing that words can be broken down into meaningful units is an important and powerful first step in vocabulary development. Students also need to think about this process from the other direction—to combine word parts to make words. In "combine and create" activities, students complete a variety of tasks to compose English words using the focus root. They might be asked to sort words containing the root into categories such as "words with/without prefixes." They might be asked to make sentences that contain two or more words with the root of focus. These activities help students identify roots and build connections between roots and the words that contain them.

For example, a "combine and create" lesson for *struct* asks students to complete a matrix with prefixes down one side and three versions of the base, some combined with suffixes (*struct, struction, structive*), across the top. Student pairs should complete the matrix. Think for a moment about the learning that is embedded in this task: students consider the "build" aspect of *struct*, to be sure, but they also think and talk about another layer of the relationships among terms—that *struct* words have important differences as well as similarities. Research tells us that this focus on similarities and differences is very powerful in promoting learning (Marzano, Pickering, and Pollock 2001).

Combine and Create

Directions: Work in pairs to build words with the *struct* base. You will complete every box.

PREFIXES	*struct*	*struction*	*structive*
con–			
de–			
in–			
ob–			

EXTEND AND EXPLORE

We want to give students multiple opportunities to think about and play with the roots we teach them. We hope that our instruction will foster an awareness of and interest in words. Open-ended activities that feature student collaboration achieve this goal nicely. The final routine in the instructional cycle, "extend and explore," has two goals. In the short term, we hope to foster additional learning about the root that is the focus of the lesson. In the long term, we want to create lifelong word lovers. Word play (riddles) and games, sketching, and other divergent-thinking activities can contribute to both goals. In addition, two- and three-word phrases that include words built on the root can be used (e.g., "under construction," "destruction of property," "constructive criticism," "obstruction in the drain"). "Flexing" words by changing suffixes can also be fun (e.g., *instruct, instructor, instructional, instructive*). (See Chapter 6 for practice and enrichment activities.)

Then what? You begin again, using a new root. You can go through this instructional cycle repeatedly, complete with the five routines, to create a structure for your vocabulary program. Then, there are two additional issues to consider and implement—how to differentiate instruction and how to assess.

Differentiating Instruction

If you are like most teachers, the range of vocabulary levels among students in your classroom is broad. You want a curriculum that is efficient, yet you also want to offer students instruction and practice that provides the best opportunity for them to learn. Teaching must be differentiated to better meet students' needs (Blachowicz and Fisher 2015).

It goes without saying that the goal is for every student to be successful. We all learn more easily when we are effectively engaged—where our motivation, curiosity, and interests are leading the learning. Now, think about the opposite—situations that do not lead to successful learning, either because the activities are too difficult or too easy or because a student is learning the language. If activities are too challenging or language barriers get in the way, we may become frustrated and think that understanding will forever be impossible. If activities are too easy, we become bored. None of these situations leads to the achievement of our long-term goals for students as word learners. We want all students to be successful all the time.

A curiosity-filled environment is one good way to foster this goal. Moreover, in the case of vocabulary learning, we want to entice students to become word lovers (lexophiles) for life, which both success and curiosity can foster. Words and language are inherently interesting!

You want to challenge students to grow and support their efforts. Pushing students toward productive struggle encourages a growth mindset. But too much challenge, or challenge without the appropriate support, is frustrating. And frustration can lead to feelings of failure. Instruction and practice should challenge students to grow and also offer the support they need to be successful.

With some creativity, many lessons can be adapted for above-level, below-level, and English learner support. The Teacher's Guide and Digital Resources for each level of the *Building Vocabulary* curriculum offers some suggestions for you to consider. Here are a few ways to differentiate, again using the *struct* instructional cycle.

Did You Know?

Words and language are inherently interesting! Entice students to become word lovers (lexophiles) for life by creating regular opportunities for them to explore new words and use them in a variety of oral and written contexts.

FOR STUDENTS WHO STRUGGLE: EXTRA SUPPORT

Working in pairs makes learning fun and also provides extra support for students who need it. Even as adults, when we work alone, it can sometimes feel as though we are being tested. Working together with someone else hardly ever feels evaluatory. Pairs can serve as recorders, for example, or a partner can support a struggling learner through quiet conversation that might include additional examples or explanations.

Some of the most helpful ways to differentiate for below-level support include providing visuals, offering additional examples with thorough explanations, and creating extra time to preview the lesson and words in advance.

If students need additional practice to understand the thinking behind "divide and conquer," provide several words featuring the focus root of the instructional cycle. Here are several for *struct*: *construct, constructed, constructing, instruct, instruction*. You can find these extra words containing each root by going to **onelook.com**, entering "*struct*" (the root with asterisks before and after), and selecting the "common words only" search. You'll get more words than you need, but skimming the list is easy.

Students can keep vocabulary journals and devote a few pages to each root, perhaps including its meaning and several key words that contain it. It may help to break some of these words apart, as in "divide and conquer": *construction* = *con–* ("with, together") + *struct* ("build") + *–ion* ("thing, act") = "something built out of parts put together," "the act of building by putting parts together." When students find *struct* words in their reading, they can add them to the appropriate journal page.

Did You Know?

If you have English learners in your classroom, we bet many of them share Spanish as a first language. In the *Building Vocabulary* curriculum, we have provided Spanish cognates for nearly all the roots under study to make use of this natural language connection. For example, here are some Spanish-English cognates with the base *struct* to share with students: *construir* (construct); *construcción* (construction); *destrucción* (destruction); *estructura* (structure); *instructor* (instructor); *instrucción* (instruction); *reconstruir* (reconstruct).

FOR ADVANCED STUDENTS: EXTRA CHALLENGE

The resource **onelook.com** comes in handy for advanced support as well. The "common words only" search on "struct" yields 94 words. What could students do with these? They could select some words from this list and make crossword puzzles or word searches (see Appendices A and B for online resources). They could make riddles for others to solve. They could look for opposites (e.g., *structured–unstructured*; *superstructure–substructure*). They could sort words by syllables or in some other way. With some imagination, you and your students will find numerous ways to support above-level learning that don't feel like extra work.

Students can use online resources (see Appendix A) to learn more about words of interest. From the "struct" search, you might want to ask them to find out about *obstructionists* or *constructivism*, for example. Or you might simply ask students to select several words that they find interesting and find out more about them.

ENGLISH LEARNER SUPPORT: MAKE COGNATE CONNECTIONS

Earlier in this book, we defined *cognates* as words that share a common root. Cognates can also be words in two languages that share similar meanings, spellings, and pronunciations (e.g., the Spanish word for *cafeteria* is *cafetería*; the Spanish word for *appetite* is *apetito*). More than 20,000 English words—30–40 percent of the English lexicon—have direct Spanish cognates. Bilingual students aware of cognate relationships do better on measures of word analysis, reading comprehension, and vocabulary in English (Nagy et al. 1993). If you have English learners in your classroom, we bet many of them share Spanish as a first language. In the *Building Vocabulary* curriculum, we have provided Spanish cognates for nearly all the roots under study to make use of this natural language connection.

Basing vocabulary instruction on cognates allows students to build bridges from Spanish to English. In essence, this approach says to Spanish-speaking students, "You already know this (Spanish) word. You can use this knowledge in English too!" In addition to focusing on the information that cognates provide, this demonstrates that we value students' home languages.

In addition to highlighting cognate connections, instructional modifications can support English learners. EL students need to focus on meaning, using research-based strategies to work with new words. They need frequent opportunities to try out new words in varied learning contexts. Adding context to the language is one of the most important keys to success for EL students. Provide sentences to go with the words you are teaching for the lesson. Try to reduce the number of words or word roots, too, since EL students may need more time to work through the activities. It is also a good idea to read the sentences or words aloud. Hearing the words will increase their verbal interaction, and they can relate the sounds to the written words.

EL students generally need more distinctive and frequent support. Pre-teach lessons with EL students so they understand the meanings of the word roots. Then, class discussion will support further comprehension and word learning. For a more in-depth discussion of English learners, see pages 24–25 in Chapter 1.

To make activities most effective, teachers can differentiate some aspects of a lesson. Not all students need to be engaged in the same activity at the same time (Reutzel and Cooter 2015). Differentiating instruction is important, but doing so doesn't mean that different groups of students need to work with different roots. The adaptations provided above can easily be integrated into the overall instructional cycle so that the classroom community can share some instructional time. Yet, with these adaptations, everyone is challenged, everyone is supported, and, most importantly, everyone can be successful.

Vocabulary Assessment

One aspect of effective vocabulary instruction is the assessment that accompanies it. We want to know that students' active and passive vocabularies are growing. Unfortunately, assessing students' vocabularies is a difficult task. According to Pearson, Hiebert, and Kamil, "our measures of vocabulary are inadequate to the challenge of documenting the relationship between word learning and global measures of comprehension" (2007, 283).

Until the research community develops a single, accurate vocabulary assessment, we need to continue using a combination of informal assessment measures. Each level of the *Building Vocabulary* curriculum contains a vocabulary pretest and posttest that focus on some word families or roots addressed at that level. Lesson reviews and unit quizzes are also provided, and activities that can serve as informal assessments are identified.

You may be interested in more general vocabulary assessments. Here are some additional assessments to try. Keep in mind that none of these offers a complete picture of students' word learning, but each adds information that allows you to see a more complete picture.

1. Cloze assessments are an easy way to assess students' understanding of target words in the context of authentic reading. To make a cloze assessment, you need to create a short passage that contains 8 to 10 words that belong to the list of words under study. Then, remove those words, and replace them with blanks. Provide students with the words they are to use, and instruct them to fill in the blanks with the appropriate words to fit the meaning of the passage. In a cloze assessment, generally a score of 75 percent correct or better is an indication that students have an adequate degree of mastery over the root and related words. After students complete a cloze, discuss with them how they were able to choose the correct words for each blank. (**Note:** Ensure there is enough context in the remaining words of the sentence or surrounding sentences to use when determining the correct missing word.)

2. When you confer with students and listen to them read, select several words from the text selection. Ask students to define the words or use them in sentences that show their meanings. Judge student success with a three-point rubric: outstanding, satisfactory, unsatisfactory (O-S-U). Unsatisfactory responses are either clearly wrong or absent, as in a student indicating that they don't know what a word means. The difference between "satisfactory" and "outstanding" is a matter of degree—outstanding responses tend to be more elaborate or offer extended examples. You can keep track of students' performance anecdotally or by using a simple two-column chart with the titles "Word" and "Rating." You can even return to words initially rated "satisfactory" or "unsatisfactory" at a later time to see whether student knowledge of the words in question has deepened.

3. Ask students to make lists of special words from their unaided writing. Look at these lists, and evaluate the sophistication of the words using the O-S-U scale.

4. Use Knowledge Rating Charts. Select key words from a text students will read. Make a three-column chart for students to indicate whether they know a word well, have seen or heard it, or do not know it at all. Blachowicz and Fisher (2015) note that this activity also helps students understand that learning the meaning of a word is a gradual process. Of course, perusing students' responses can provide assessment information as well. Here is a sample chart using a few words from this paragraph:

WORD	KNOW IT WELL	HAVE SEEN IT OR HEARD IT	DO NOT KNOW IT AT ALL
knowledge			
activity			
understand			

Using a student's chart for assessment purposes means that you trust the student has answered thoughtfully. Nonetheless, what could you learn if a student marked that they knew every word well? What could you do to quickly check a student's perceptions of word knowledge?

5. Encourage self-assessment. Students can—and should—have some say in evaluating their own vocabulary growth. In addition to fostering students' sense of responsibility for their own learning, self-assessment is often motivating. Furthermore, self-assessment sends a subtle reminder about the importance of words and word learning. Each time they assess themselves, students will think about vocabulary as an abstract concept. Over time, they will think about "word awareness" as they read. You might challenge students to write about their own word knowledge in their journals, for example. Or have them write definitions of new concepts in their own words to reflect more broadly on the new words they have learned or on the value of word learning. Ask them to describe where they find new and interesting words. Ask them to identify which strategies they use most often to figure out the meanings of new words (Newton, Padak, and Rasinski 2008).

SUMMARY

We hope you have found this chapter *instructive* with regard to the *instructional* basics. Vocabulary teaching and learning requires making judgments about how to use time and develop instructional routines from a gradual release of responsibility model. Against this framework, you can teach, assess, and differentiate your instruction to support every learner's needs. As we often note, the ultimate goal is for students to become independent, curious, and strategic word sleuths. As you move your students toward this goal, we hope your vocabulary *instruction* will be full of success and fun for your students and you, the *instructor*.

CHAPTER 6

Vocabulary Practice Activities

Practice makes perfect. We've all heard it. Practice helps us learn new skills, such as perfecting an accurate tennis swing, learning to read sheet music, or driving a car. Practice allows us to become comfortable with a complex activity and to participate in it without thinking about its individual parts. We learn how to coordinate and integrate the parts of the skill into the whole. So, what about vocabulary practice? What should students do to practice vocabulary, and what should they practice? What characterizes a good practice activity for vocabulary learning?

First, it is based on the instructional principles outlined in Chapter 1. These instructional principles focus on what students need in order to learn. When you ground your teaching in what students need, you maximize the impact of instructional time. Use the instructional principles to guide your decisions about what to teach and how to teach it. The following principles and instructional methods are particularly important.

	Students need... strategies for determining word meaning that will help them with metacognitive and metalinguistic awareness (Nagy and Scott 2000)—becoming aware of their own thinking and language processes.
	Teachers can... demonstrate how to use Greek and Latin roots to figure out the meaning and usage of new words and provide practice opportunities through independent and shared reading and discussion about words.
	Students need... to be immersed in words, with frequent opportunities to use new words in diverse oral and print contexts in order to learn them on a deep level (Blachowicz and Fisher 2002, 2006).
	Teachers can... create word-rich learning environments with instructional routines such as graffiti walls, word-play activities, and shared and independent reading.
	Students need... to develop word consciousness, an awareness of and interest in words (Graves and Watts-Taffe 2002).
	Teachers can... model enthusiasm for words and engage students in a variety of word-play strategies to foster curiosity about words.

When we ground our teaching in these instructional principles, we engage students in vocabulary practice that is purposeful, authentic, enjoyable, engaging, and likely to lead to gains in word knowledge and word awareness.

But what should this vocabulary practice look like? Consider the example of learning to drive a car. One important criterion is difficulty level—we would not ask a new driver to negotiate an expressway during rush hour. Another criterion is support, or scaffolding. Parents or driving instructors ride along with novice drivers. And probably the most important criterion is authenticity—someone who wants to learn to drive must eventually hit the streets. These three criteria—difficulty level, support or scaffolding, and authenticity—apply to vocabulary practice.

The criterion of difficulty level, applied to vocabulary practice, suggests the need to differentiate. Students may complete the same activity but with different words or word parts, or they may engage in independent reading with texts suited to their own unique interests. After all, in a class of 25 or more students, it doesn't make much sense to assume that everyone needs to practice the same things. Think about your English learners, students working above level, and students who are still working toward proficiency: What accommodations can you make for them?

Just as you would support a novice driver by riding alongside as they learn to navigate rush-hour traffic, you also provide support for your students as they learn about words. This support can come from you through modeling activities, leading discussions about words, demonstrating how to use Greek and Latin roots to figure out new words, and showing enthusiasm for and interest in words. Support can also come from peers. When student pairs work through an activity together, they often teach each other as they talk about words, draw attention to parts of words others may not notice, and expand their receptive and expressive vocabularies.

Authenticity matters. Ultimately, we learn vocabulary by reading and talking with others. Therefore, to be effective, vocabulary instruction must include purposeful and authentic opportunities for students to read, write, and talk with others every day (Newton 2018). When teaching novice drivers, we make sure they have chances to drive in real traffic situations so they can integrate multiple skills, including how to reverse, merge, and change lanes. When teaching students vocabulary, we make sure they have many chances to read, write, listen, and speak so they can orchestrate their receptive and expressive vocabularies and use words to understand and be understood. Provide time every day for students to read, write, listen, and speak.

Did You Know?

Students should rarely, if ever, work in isolation when learning about words. Practice that does not incorporate talk or time with text is unlikely to result in vocabulary understanding. To maximize the impact of vocabulary instruction, find opportunities to replace solitary worksheets, vocabulary packets, or flash cards with authentic word-learning experiences that center on authentic reading and rich oral discussion.

Students should rarely—if ever—work in isolation when learning about words. Practice that does not incorporate talk or time with text is unlikely to result in deep vocabulary understanding. To maximize the impact of your vocabulary instruction, find places where you can replace solitary worksheets, vocabulary packets, and flash cards (if you are using these methods) with authentic word-learning experiences that center on authentic reading and rich talk.

The classroom-tested strategies that follow are based on the instructional principles for word learning. They include opportunities for talk about and exploration of words in meaningful and diverse contexts. We have used these activities successfully in our own work with students, and we know dozens of teachers who have done likewise. The format for each description is similar: purpose, materials, general procedures, and adaptations for different situations or groups of learners. The key to the following instructional routines lies in the opportunities to engage with words in authentic reading experiences and in the talk between peers and with a teacher. Make decisions about how to adapt practice opportunities to best fit students' strengths and needs as word learners.

Text-Based Practice Activities

Since reading is a key element of effective vocabulary instruction, the first practice activities outlined center on rich and authentic reading experiences. In the following suggestions, notice how we have intentionally incorporated practice with roots-based strategies into familiar activities. By doing this, students will be exploring new words—and building vocabulary—as a natural part of the reading process.

DAILY INDEPENDENT READING

Daily independent reading is an integral part of vocabulary learning. Setting up a consistent independent-reading routine in your classroom ensures that students have time and opportunities to engage with academic vocabulary. Since books are chock-full of words with Greek and Latin roots, the more time students spend reading, the more opportunities they have to build their proficiency with Greek and Latin roots. Reading volume and variety are particularly important when developing vocabulary knowledge. Create opportunities for your students to read widely about a range of topics that spark their interests. As students read independently, conduct reading conferences.

Build and maintain a well-stocked and well-organized classroom library. Aim for a minimum of 10 books per student (Reutzel and Fawson 2002), and eventually work up to the recommended library size of 700 to 750 books (Allington and Cunningham 2001). Build your collection gradually, making sure to include a variety of genres, graphic novels, magazines, and books at multiple reading levels. Ensure that the titles in your library represent students' diverse experiences, cultures, and perspectives. Organize the books in ways that are inviting to students and easy for them to access.

Develop a system for jotting notes while you confer with students. An organized system for taking notes will help you track what you observe students are doing when they come to unknown words as well as provide you with a record of when you met with each student.

General Procedures

1. Schedule time every day for students to read a variety of self-selected books, magazines, poems, and other texts that draw their interests. This will be a time when all students are reading independently.

2. As students read, conduct individual and small-group reading conferences. As you confer with students, notice what they do when they come to words that are new to them. Teach or revisit how to use known Greek and Latin roots to decode multisyllabic words and to figure out what unfamiliar words might mean. For example, if students are trying to understand the word *subterranean*, prompt them to use what they know about the prefix *sub–* or the base *terr* as a way into the word.

3. We have found the following prompts helpful for both teacher-led modeling and guided practice when working with students:

   - Find a prefix, a suffix, or a base that you know. Use the meaning to think about what the whole word might mean.

   - Think of a word you know that has the same prefix, suffix, or base. Use what you know about that word in this context to determine what this word might mean.

4. Use what you observe to identify areas of strength and need for your students. Use these trends to determine which roots and word-solving strategies you may need to reteach in whole- or small-group settings.

5. Students need ample time every day to read independently. Give students time to talk about what they read every day too. In addition to allotting time to discuss their thinking and ideas about what they are reading, include a few minutes one or two times a week for students to share interesting or confusing words they came across while reading.

Adaptations

- The amount of time you allot for independent reading will vary throughout the year as students' reading stamina develops. Scaffold independent reading by beginning with small amounts of time, gradually increasing independent reading time as students demonstrate greater stamina.

- To build vocabulary knowledge, students should read texts that they are interested in and that include a substantial number of new words. Help students find books that may be a little challenging but will not frustrate them. If you notice that students consistently read texts that contain few new words, use reading conferences to guide them toward more challenging texts that may be of interest. Teach and revisit word-solving strategies students can use to figure out new words as they read more sophisticated texts.

SHARED READING

Shared reading is a method for modeling word-analysis skills and word consciousness. Reading a text together with students provides opportunities for context-based inquiry about a root. This routine expands students' vocabulary knowledge by exposing them to a wide array of words. Class messages, such as the morning or daily message, are ideal ways to provide students with authentic, text-based opportunities to develop vocabulary knowledge and word-analysis skills.

General Procedures

1. Craft a brief message to share with your students. Create the content of the message so that it includes a few words with the root being studied. You do not need to overload the message with root words; just two to three words will do the trick. See below for an example of a message with the prefix re– ("back, again").

> Dear Students,
>
> Today, we will discuss our ideas about characters and discover what other students think. Some of us might even revise our thinking! Today, we return our library books. Will you check out a new book or renew a favorite?

2. Display the message so that all students can see it.

3. Read the message aloud to students as they read it silently.

4. Think aloud about the contents of the message, focusing on the aspect of vocabulary you want students to practice. For example, say, "I'm noticing that a few words in this message share an idea about something going 'back' or happening 'again,' such as the word revise, which means 'turning back or away

from old ways of thinking and considering new ideas.' Will you look at this message with me and see what you notice about words that might share the meaning of 'going back or happening again'?"

5. As students share, record the words on a chart or a word wall. Jot the words and their meanings in student-friendly language, making sure to include *back* or *again* (e.g., When we return books, we hand them "back").

6. Build on students' thinking to generate other words that might also have *re–* and mean "back" or "again." Suggested language: "We're noticing that *re–* means 'back' or 'again' and that it comes at the beginning of words. So it could be a prefix. Let's explore this idea to see whether it might be true anywhere else. What other words can you think of that might have the prefix *re–* and a meaning of 'back, again'?"

7. Prompt students to turn and talk as they generate other words they might know with *re–*. Add the words and meanings to the chart. Guide students to create a tentative generalization based on what they have noticed. For example, ask: "What are your thoughts about the prefix *re–* now?" Write students' thinking at the top of the chart: for example, *re–* is a prefix that means "back" or "again."

8. Reread the message, guiding students to think about the meaning of the root. As you close the lesson, invite students to discover words with the prefix throughout the day. For example: "We have an interesting idea about the prefix *re–*. Today as you read, write, and work, be on the lookout for words you think might fit our idea. You can jot them on sticky notes if you'd like. Bring them to our morning meeting tomorrow so we can explore them." Add these new words to your word wall.

Adaptations

- If you do not have time in your instructional day for a morning or daily message, consider other times during the day where you could devote 10–15 minutes a few times a week for shared reading with a class message. Some teachers use "Dear Scientists" or "Dear Historians" messages to launch content-area instruction, crafting the message around a root and key content-area vocabulary; other teachers use shared reading with class messages as students transition back to learning after lunch or recess. Devoting just 10–15 minutes to this routine a few times a week will help your students build vocabulary knowledge.

- Post the word wall in the classroom. Throughout the week, invite students to add words that contain the root to the chart. Allot a few minutes during the week to talk about some of the words students have added.

- Some teachers have shared that crafting messages can be challenging at first but with practice becomes easier. We have found the following reminders helpful when writing class messages:
  - Be brief. The message only has to be a few sentences long. Three to five sentences are enough.
  - Do not overload the message with root words. Two to three words are ample. Choose one word that you will use to model thinking; leave the rest for students to discover and discuss.
  - Focus on the content of the message first. We have found that when we start by thinking about what we want to say, the root words tend to fall into place. As with all writing, craft the message around meaning, then tweak to fit in vocabulary.

Activities to Build a Word-Rich Learning Environment

All the activities in this chapter will help you construct a word-rich learning environment. The activities outlined below make use of physical space to display words that students themselves find noteworthy. The accompanying instructional routines also include time for teacher-and-peer discussions.

GRAFFITI WALLS

Graffiti walls are student-created, interactive word walls. Graffiti walls are crafted by students and feature words with roots they have discovered. After the graffiti wall has been created, the teacher leads a discussion about some of the words on the wall. This instructional strategy creates a space for students and teachers to connect with academic language in an engaging and authentic way.

General Procedures

1. Post a large, blank sheet of paper where students can easily write on it. Some teachers tape a sheet of paper on a counter in the classroom. Others designate a whiteboard or use painters' tape to section off a small portion of the whiteboard for the graffiti wall.

2. Place a tub of markers next to the chart or whiteboard.

3. Write the root students are studying and its meaning on the chart. You can write the root in the center of the paper or at the top; just be sure to include both the root and its meaning.

4. Over the course of several days, invite and encourage students to add words they find that might fit the root (as well as synonyms to the words they find). Some teachers have found it helpful to talk with students about times during the day when they can add to the wall and times when it may be disruptive. One fifth-grade teacher we worked with allotted three minutes at the end of the independent block for students to add to the wall; a second-grade teacher added graffiti wall time as part of students' morning routine.

5. Once the graffiti wall is full of words, facilitate a brief class discussion about a few of the words. Use this discussion to clarify misconceptions, explore words students are curious about, talk about literal and figurative meanings, discuss and sort words to determine whether they contain the roots or are false etymologies, or other aspects of the root/words that students have expressed interest in. (For more information on false etymologies, see Chapter 8.)

6. Hang the completed graffiti wall in the classroom where students can easily see it. Encourage them to use and add to it regularly.

Adaptations

- If students prefer to see words in a more organized manner, direct them to write words on sticky notes. One teacher found it helpful to spend a few minutes rewriting students' words on fresh sticky notes in dark, clear lettering before class discussions. During class discussions, her students work together to sort the words into categories they generate. The teacher reports that students enjoy the act of physically moving and reordering the sticky notes. As a result of cooperatively organizing the words and the dark, clear lettering, students are better able to find words on the graffiti wall.

- If you have limited wall space, take a photo of the completed class graffiti wall. Make copies of the photo for students to post in their word journals as a reference.

WORDS WE ARE CURIOUS ABOUT

As you create time and space for students to practice with vocabulary, students' curiosity about words will ignite. Teachers we have worked with have, quite happily, discovered that as students' enthusiasm for words increases, they become more aware of words they want to explore. Sometimes, there is not enough time in the day to discuss the plethora of new words students are curious about. Sometimes—because we are all word learners—students pose questions about words that we as teachers are not quite sure how to answer. Here, a simple *Words We Are Curious About* chart can come in quite handy.

General Procedures

1. Place a blank sheet of paper somewhere students can access it easily. Write *Words We Are Curious About* at the top of the paper. Place a tub of markers nearby.

2. When time is tight or when students broach words about which you yourself are unsure, ask them to write these words on the chart. Be sure to add words that you are curious about or that you think your students may find interesting (e.g., *pseudonym, photosynthesis, auditorium, migration* vs. *immigration* vs. *emigration*).

3. Invite students to become word researchers and explore the meanings of these words on their own. **Note:** A few lessons on how to use online dictionaries and other simple reference materials, such as glossaries, will be necessary for students to be successful word researchers. (See Appendix A for resources.)

4. As time permits, invite students to share what they learned with their classmates.

Adaptations

Designate a section of students' Reader's or Writer's Notebooks where they can jot down words they would like to learn more about. As part of students' reading and/or writing routines, allocate a few minutes once or twice a week for them to research and record what they learn about these words.

Word-Analysis Strategies

Use the following strategies to help students use their knowledge of Greek and Latin roots to determine the meanings of unfamiliar words. These strategies develop students' metalinguistic awareness—the understanding of how words work—as well as their ability to analyze words to unlock meaning. Chapter 5 described two other powerful practice activities: Word Spokes and Divide and Conquer. In the *Building Vocabulary* curriculum, these are used for instruction, but when students learn the routines, they can be useful for practice as well. The "divide and conquer" routine also works well during reading conferences.

SEMANTIC FEATURE ANALYSIS

Semantic Feature Analysis (SFA) is another way for students to visualize similarities and differences among related words. The visual is a chart. The rows on the chart list several related words. The columns list qualities or characteristics. Students complete their charts considering whether each term reflects each of the qualities or characteristics. Here is an example using words from a lesson about two-syllable compound words.

	MEANS OF TRANSPORTATION	SOMETHING PLEASANT	DONE OUTSIDE	INVOLVES EATING
airplane	+	+	+	−
baseball	−	+	+	−
homework	−	−	−	−
sailboat	+	+	+	−
oatmeal	−	+/−	−	+
birthday	−	+	+/−	+
playground	−	+	+	−

General Procedures

1. Create an SFA table, such as the one above. Choose 8 to 10 words from the lesson (preferably nouns). Write each word in the left-hand column.

2. Make a copy of the template with words for each student. Then, as a group or as individuals, have students think of features or characteristics that would differentiate one or some of the words from others. List each feature on the top row of the template.

3. Have students work to fill in the template, answering yes/no (+/−) for each word and feature.

4. When complete, have students discuss how they answered each column.

Adaptations

- Students can work individually, in pairs, or in small groups.

- Use images in place of the words.

- Students can develop definitions for the words using the features.

- If students are unsure about how to complete portions of the chart, they can research answers.

- If features or characteristics do not lend themselves to yes/no responses, you can ask students to respond using a 5-point scale (1 = definitely no; 3 = somewhat; 5 = definitely yes).

- Include a blank column so that students can think of new feature for words that have identical features in the original analysis.

ODD WORD OUT

One way to make the meaning of a word clear is to compare how similar to, or different from, other words it is. This quick activity asks students to choose which word does not "fit" and then to explain why. It promotes classification, analysis, and creative thinking about words. Student pairs can work together. Their discussion of responses will be enriching. If students are all working on the same sets of words, whole-group conversation can conclude the activity.

To prepare the activity, assemble sets of four words, three of which can be grouped together for some reason, with the remaining word being the "odd word out." This activity can be found throughout the *Building Vocabulary from Word Roots* curriculum, or you can make activity sheets for students.

Odd Word Out

Directions: Look at the four words. On the first line, write the word that doesn't belong. Then, explain how the other words are similar.

precook	preheat	premixed	pretest

The word that doesn't belong is _____.

The other words are similar because _____.

prehistoric	preshrink	presoak	prewash

The word that doesn't belong is _____.

The other words are similar because _____.

pregame	predict	pressure	precaution

The word that doesn't belong is _____.

The other words are similar because _____.

The groups of words you select for Odd Word Out will often have multiple answers, which will promote students' divergent thinking about the many ways in which words can be related to one another. In the first set of words, for example, the "odd word" could be *pretest* because the remaining words relate to cooking. Or the odd word could be *premixed* because it is the only word with an *–ed* ending. Or it could even be *preheat*, since it is the only word with a long vowel sound. It is almost better if more than one odd word can be found because it makes the activity more interesting for students.

General Procedures

1. If the activity is new to students, you will need to introduce it. It may help to show students a set of four words and then think aloud about how you might select the odd word. For example, you might write *cat*, *dog*, *turtle*, and *lion* on the board. Then, you could think aloud: "The odd word could be *lion* because the other three could be pets, or because it is the only word with a long vowel sound. Or the odd word could be *turtle* because it is the only one that lives in water, or because the other three are mammals." The idea is to help students see possibilities.

2. After you have demonstrated the activity, provide another set (or two) of words, and ask student pairs to figure out the odd word. Invite whole-group sharing. Be sure to ask students to explain their reasoning. Continue until you know that students understand the thinking process.

3. Provide students with four to five sets of words. Each student pair should figure out the odd words. Conclude with a sharing discussion, as above.

Adaptations

- You can differentiate instruction by providing students with different sets of words based on student ability.

- You can provide extra support for students by leading the discussion that is aimed toward finding the odd word. If you do this, be sure to ask questions that encourage student thinking rather than provide the correct answers.

- Students can share their words with another group without indicating their reasons for choosing the odd word. The other group tries to figure out which is the odd word.

- You can invite student pairs to examine the class word wall to create their own sets of four words. They can explain their odd-word choices to you or, better yet, give the sets to other students to solve.

WORD SORTS

Any activity that asks students to organize or categorize words could be called a "word sort." The purpose of any word sort activity is for students to think about different aspects of words, what the words have in common, and how they relate to a text that students have read.

General Procedures

1. Select about 20 words for sorting. For example, you might select words that have prefixes, suffixes, or both; words that start the same but have or do not have prefixes (e.g., *preheat, press*); or words from a text that students will read or have read. Write the words on individual cards or slips of paper. If you are introducing word sorts to students, you may also want to print the words on strips of paper so that you can demonstrate the process of sorting the word strips.

2. Provide one set of word cards to each pair of students. Ask students to group the words. Remind them that they will be asked to explain their groupings. Consider the following criteria when grouping words:

   - presence or absence of a prefix, base, or suffix
   - presence or absence of a particular root
   - number of syllables
   - presence or absence of a particular vowel or consonant sound

3. After a few minutes, invite students to discuss one of their groupings, both the words contained in it and their reasons for putting those words together.

Adaptations

- If time permits, have students sort the same set of words repeatedly (e.g., by the presence or absence of a word part, by number of syllables). Each sort provides students with another opportunity to think about both the words and their component parts.

- If you have drawn words from a text that students will read, ask them to sort by text-related categories (e.g., characters, plot, setting). Be sure students understand that they are making good guesses and not finding the right answers, since they have not yet read the text. After reading, invite students to return to their groupings and alter them based on the text.

- Use sorts to determine whether words contain roots or are false etymologies. In a third-grade class, the teacher noticed that the graffiti wall contained words such as *uncle* and *under*, examples of false etymologies, when students were learning about the prefix *un–* meaning "not." She guided the class to sort the words on the graffiti wall. Students considered whether the words on the wall had the meaning of "not." Words that did have a meaning of "not" were placed under the category "Contains the Prefix." Words that did not have a meaning of "not," such as *uncle* and *under*, were placed under the category "Does Not Contain the Prefix."

- Instead of using word cards, you can write the words on a sheet of paper for each student. Then, have students do the sort by writing the words on separate sheets of paper on which they have drawn columns that represent individual categories.

Word-Play Activities

The activities below expand students' vocabulary knowledge using word games. Through these games, students deepen word knowledge by exploring gradations of meaning, building semantic connections between words, and broadening receptive and expressive vocabulary with rich peer and teacher talk.

WORD THEATER

This versatile strategy, based on the game of Charades, uses pantomime and oral language to make word meanings concrete. Its purpose is to help students build or reinforce conceptual knowledge by acting out the meaning of a new or familiar vocabulary word. Word Theater works especially well as a partner or small-group activity.

General Procedures

1. List 10 words that share a root on the board. Be sure that the words can be dramatized easily.

2. Have each student read the list of words aloud to a partner. When both students have read the list, they should secretly choose a word. Tell them they have two minutes to decide how to demonstrate the word's meaning by acting it out without speaking.

3. Now, ask each team to mime its word while other students try to guess the word. Keep the list of words visible so that the audience can keep rereading the words as they try to figure out which one is being acted out. As students look for connections between the acting and the word list, they will better understand the concepts each word represents.

Adaptations

- Peer tutors or adult volunteers can provide below-level support. Allow additional time for students to decide on their pantomimes. The assistant should encourage talk about the selected word as well as the actions that will become the pantomime.

- Two sets of student pairs can work together if their words are related in some way. Then, they can present both pantomimes together.

- Have students draw sketches instead of pantomiming.

- Word Skits work well with students who are both experienced in pantomiming words and comfortable working in small teams of three to four. Each team chooses one word and writes its definition on an index card. Working together, they create a skit or a situation that shows the meaning of the word. The skit is performed without words. Classmates try to guess the word being shown. Once the word is correctly identified, the definition is read out loud.

WORDO

This vocabulary version of Bingo is a wonderful way for students to play with new words and experience the words through simultaneous use of oral and written language. Create a list of 9–25 words based on the grade level; these may contain the same root, be related in some other way, or be randomly selected. Prepare a clue for each word. The clue can be a definition, a synonym, an antonym, or a sentence with the target word deleted. The clues can even be a bit more complex (e.g., a word that begins with a prefix, has three syllables, and contains a consonant blend). You can print copies of premade matrices from **www.timrasinski.com** under the resources tab. (Create a three-by-three, four-by-four, or five-by-five square matrix, and ensure the squares are large enough for students to write in.) Provide a copy of the Wordo card you choose to each student. Supply students with movable markers of some sort—dry beans, pennies, or scraps of paper—so they can reuse their Wordo cards.

General Procedures

1. Write the words you have chosen on the board.

2. Provide a Wordo card for each student. Ask each student to choose a free box and mark it with an X. Then, have them choose words from the list on the board and write one word in each of the remaining boxes. Students can fill in any word in any box they choose.

3. Read a clue for each word.

4. Students mark the target word on their boards. When a student has filled a row, a column, a diagonal, or four corners, they can call out, "Wordo!"

5. Confirm that the winner accurately identified the target words. Have students clear their sheets and play another round. The winner of the first game can call out clues for the second game.

Adaptations

- Play Wordo several times with the same set of words. For example, you can play a round using definitions as clues, then another round with synonyms as clues. Afterward, engage students in discussion about which types of clues were most helpful.

- Small groups of students can select words and develop clues. Then, one group can lead Wordo for classmates.

20 QUESTIONS

The vocabulary version of this popular game uses oral language and personal connections to deepen conceptual knowledge. Students take turns asking questions that help them figure out a "mystery" word. If you want to build a little competitive spirit, you can divide the class into two teams for this activity. You will need a paper bag with at least a dozen slips of paper featuring words with the given root.

General Procedures

1. If students have never played 20 Questions, review the rules with them. Tell students that one of them will get to be "it." This student will choose a word that classmates will try to guess by asking questions. If no one can figure out the word after 20 questions have been asked, then the student who is "it" will reveal the word.

2. If someone guesses the correct word, that person becomes "it" and gets to choose the next word. Remind students that the person who is "it" can only give yes or no answers to the questions.

3. You may want to scaffold this by taking the first turn as "it" yourself. Otherwise, invite someone to begin by selecting a word from the bag. Then, let students take over and ask questions until someone has guessed the correct word.

4. Repeat the process. This game can take as much or as little time as you choose. It is good as a quick filler or a Friday afternoon wind-down activity.

Adaptations

- You can change the number of questions that students ask; that is, you can play 15 Questions instead of 20 Questions, for example.

- Two students can be "it" simultaneously and can confer before answering questions. This is a good adaptation to provide support for English learners.

ROOT-WORD RIDDLES

This activity invites students to create and figure out riddles about words with the same root. Students guess the word by connecting clues. This works well as a student-pair or a team activity.

General Procedures

1. Create a list of 10 words that contain the same root. Begin by reviewing the meaning of the root. Read the list of words together. Ask students to explain what each word means. Make sure their explanations include the meaning of the root.

2. If students have not created riddles before, share some riddles with them. Visit **brownielocks.com/riddles.html**, which contains examples of riddles. Spend some time not only solving riddles but also talking about how riddles are constructed. Ask students what kinds of clues seem particularly helpful.

3. Choose a word from the list. Tell students you are going to create a riddle for them to figure out and that they will get three clues. Write the first clue. Make sure to begin it with the words *I mean* (e.g., for the word *invisible*: I mean "something you cannot see").

4. Write a second and third clue (e.g., My opposite is *visible*; I have four syllables). End with the question "What am I?"

5. Ask student pairs to choose a word from the list and make their own riddles to share with the class.

6. Finally, spend some time swapping riddles. When students have written riddles about the same word, point out the variety of clues and ways in which the word can be described.

Adaptations

- Students can make riddle books, perhaps by root or by word part (e.g., "Our Riddle Book of Prefixes"). These books can be added to the classroom library.

- Extra time, pair-work opportunities, and scaffolded tasks can provide below-level support.

- Students can take their riddles home for family members to solve.

- Older students can make riddles for younger students and share them via school mail or email.

Card Games

Card games such as Memory or Concentration, War, and Go Fish are engaging independent activities. Students can play these games with decks of word cards.

MEMORY OR CONCENTRATION

General Procedures

1. The object of this game is to find two word cards that match. To play, students will need pairs of cards with the same word, root, or word part on them. Pairs or small groups of three or four students can play this game.

2. Students should shuffle the deck of word cards and then place them facedown. You might suggest that they make a square—four rows and four columns, for example.

3. Students take turns trying to make matches. The first student turns over two cards. If they match, the student keeps them and takes another turn. If they do not match, the student puts them back facedown and the next student takes a turn. The student with the most cards when all matches have been found wins the game.

Adaptations

- Students can make matches in a variety of ways:

   1. A prefix (or a suffix) and a base word that go together to make a real word (e.g., *pre–* + *game* = *pregame* would be a match; *pre–* + *dog* = *predog* would not). You can also use words that can become compound words (e.g., *base* + *ball*) or that cannot become compound words (e.g., *base* + *lawn*).

   2. Words that contain the same root (e.g., *container, abstain; pretest, preheat; look, looking*) challenge students by asking them to identify what the word part is or what it means.

   3. You can pair individual words with cards that have their definitions, synonyms, or other clues.

- You can make the activity easier or more difficult by using different words and word parts.

WORD WAR

General Procedures

1. Assemble a large deck of word cards by using brainstormed lists of words that contain certain roots (e.g., *pre–* words or *tri* words). This game can be played with two to four students. You will need at least 10 word cards per student.

2. Deal the entire deck of word cards evenly among students. (If there are leftover cards, set them aside.)

3. Each player turns a card over and says the word and its meaning. Then, all players count the letters in the word. The player with the longest word wins all the cards. Play resumes with each player turning over another card.

4. If there is a tie for longest word, those players reveal an additional card, say the word, and count the letters. These "word wars" continue until someone's word is the longest, at which point that player takes all the cards that are turned over. Then, play resumes as in Step 3.

5. When all the cards have been turned over, the player with the most cards wins.

Adaptations

- Make the game easier or harder by selecting easier or more challenging words when creating the deck.

- Students who need more support can play as a team, with two students playing with one set of cards.

- You can make the game more challenging by asking students to name or define word parts instead of simply saying the words on the cards that they turn over.

- Alphabetical order rather than word length can be used to determine the winner of the round.

GO FISH

General Procedures

1. Assemble a deck of word cards that contains sets of four related words (e.g., *look, looks, looking, looked; return, rewind, rethink, refund; player, dancer, runner,*

walker). You will need about 10 cards per player. The game can be played by two to four students.

2. Deal cards so that each player has six. The remaining cards go facedown in the center of the playing area.

3. Students should sort their cards and look for related words. If dealt three or four related cards, these can be turned faceup on the table.

4. One student begins by asking another for a card to add to a set (e.g., "Do you have a card with the base word *look*?"). If the other student has a card that matches the criterion, they must give it to the student who asked.

5. The student continues asking for cards until the other student does not have one to give that fits the criterion. At this point, the other student says, "Go fish." The first student takes a card from the center of the table. If this card allows the student to make a set of three or four, these go on the table, and the student's turn continues. If not, this student's turn is over, and the next student takes a turn.

6. Play continues until one student has all their cards in sets on the table. This student is the winner.

Adaptations

- Use smaller sets of two cards to make the game easier.

- Students can make their own word cards before play begins. They can begin with a list of base words.

- Students can make matches according to prefix, suffix, or root.

Word Puzzles

Challenge students with crossword puzzles, word searches, jumbles, and word ladders. See Appendix B for websites for creating your own crossword puzzles and word searches.

CLOZE

In Chapter 5, we described cloze as an assessment technique. It is also an excellent way to model and practice using context clues to determine word meaning. Cloze activities help develop readers' understanding and use of context clues. Students predict words that have been omitted (or covered up) in a passage. To develop the activity, choose a reading selection, either fiction or nonfiction, and delete selected words. Cloze can be done independently with activity sheets prepared in advance. These are meant for informal assessment, but of course you can use them in other ways. In the *Building Vocabulary* curriculum, you will find cloze activities for all lessons in Levels 2 and up.

General Procedures

1. Select (or create) a text that will challenge but not overwhelm your students. Identify several words that may easily be predicted from the semantic context of the story. Leave the first and last sentences intact so that students have a mental framework. Cover the selected words with sticky notes, or omit the words if constructing a passage for duplication. (In a traditional cloze, every fifth word is deleted, but how many, the frequency of deletion, and which words are omitted should depend on your judgment of text difficulty and student need as well as the purpose of the lesson.)

2. Read the text to students. When you come to a covered or omitted word, finish reading the sentence before you stop. If students are reading independently, tell them to read to the end of each sentence before looking for context clues.

3. Ask students to predict each covered or omitted word. As each word is discussed, make sure that students describe the strategies they used to figure it out. This talk deepens metacognitive awareness. Point out the variety of clues that students used as well as the importance of using prior knowledge to solve the problem.

4. After you have scaffolded the cloze process several times, students will be able to complete cloze activities independently.

Adaptations

- You can develop cloze with texts that feature many examples of a particular root (e.g., many words with prefixes, a particular prefix, or a base, such as *tain*).

- You can provide clues for deleted words (e.g., beginning sounds, base words).

- Multiple-choice cloze (called Maze) provides students with word choices for each deletion.

- Cloze activities can be completed on computers, making them suitable for centers.

- Students can develop cloze activities for others to solve.

SCATTERGORIES

This version of the popular board game is a wonderful way to use the skill of categorization to build vocabulary. The purpose of the game is to broaden students' conceptual knowledge by connecting vocabulary words to specific categories. This works especially well as a student-pair or team activity. To create the Scattergories matrix, put several letters along the first column and a list of three to five categories that can generate many words (e.g., vegetables, countries, animals) along the top row. The categories can be general or developed from themes or content areas. You can even leave a blank column for students to choose the category.

LETTERS	FOODS	ANIMALS	NAMES
C			
F			
T			

You can also use roots.

ROOTS	IN–/IM–	–IBLE/–ABLE	–ER/–OR
port			
vis			
flam			

General Procedures

1. Provide students with blank Scattergories matrices, or create one on the board they can copy. Provide students with the categories.

2. Give students five minutes, working individually or in teams, to think of as many words as they can that begin with the given letters (or have the given roots) and fit the categories. Remind students to write in one box all the words that they think of that begin with the same letter.

3. When time is up, ask students to share their words. The player or team with the greatest number of correct words wins.

4. After you have scaffolded this activity several times, students will be ready to play Scattergories independently.

Adaptations

- Alphaboxes (Hoyt 1999) is a variation of Scattergories that can be played in teams or as a whole group. In this version, students brainstorm a word for every letter of the alphabet. The words are related to a topic or a text that has been read. (If the topic is "animals," for example, students might brainstorm *ant*, *bear*, *cat*, *dog*, *elephant*, etc.) Students can generate as many topic-related words as they can think of for each letter.

- You can develop a Scattergories or Alphaboxes matrix for a bulletin board. Leave it up for a week, and ask students to add words as they think of them.

- Invite students to develop their own Scattergories matrices for others to solve.

Vocabulary Activities Chart

The Vocabulary Activities Chart shows how adaptable these activities can be by addressing group size, whether the activities are suitable for centers (or are better for independent work), and type of words or word parts you can use.

ACTIVITY	GROUP SIZE	SUITABLE FOR CENTERS	TYPES OF WORDS/WORD PARTS
Shared Reading	whole, small	no	prefixes, suffixes, bases
Graffiti Walls	whole	no	prefixes, suffixes, bases
Words We Are Curious About	whole	no	prefixes, suffixes, bases
Semantic Feature Analysis	whole, small	yes	compound words, nouns, general vocabulary, content-area vocabulary
Odd Word Out	small, pairs	yes	prefixes, suffixes, bases, general vocabulary, content-area vocabulary
Word Theater	whole	no	prefixes, suffixes, bases, general vocabulary, content-area vocabulary
Wordo	whole	no	prefixes, suffixes, bases, general vocabulary, content-area vocabulary
20 Questions	whole, small, pairs	no	prefixes, suffixes, bases, general vocabulary, content-area vocabulary

ACTIVITY	GROUP SIZE	SUITABLE FOR CENTERS	TYPES OF WORDS/WORD PARTS
Root Word Riddles	small, pairs	yes	prefixes, suffixes, bases, general vocabulary, content-area vocabulary
Card Games	small	yes	prefixes, suffixes, bases, general vocabulary, content-area vocabulary
Word Puzzles	pairs, individually	yes	prefixes, suffixes, bases, general vocabulary, content-area vocabulary
Cloze	pairs, individually	yes	prefixes, suffixes, bases, general vocabulary, content-area vocabulary
Scattergories	small, pairs	yes	prefixes, suffixes, bases, general vocabulary, content-area vocabulary
Word Sorts	small, pairs	yes	prefixes, suffixes, bases, general vocabulary, content-area vocabulary

SUMMARY

These activities will provide your students with interesting and engaging vocabulary practice. We recommend that you introduce one activity at a time. For English learners and struggling students, scaffold their understanding by demonstrating the activity in a whole-group setting. Continue these demonstrations until students understand how the activity proceeds. After this, students should be able to complete the activities independently. Ask advanced students to create new versions of these activities and to work with the rest of the class, modeling and assisting as needed. Be sure to survey students about the activities they find most appealing.

CHAPTER 7

Roots in Action: Classroom Snapshots

In the last chapter, we shared some effective classroom-tested instructional activities that will give your students practice with roots. We noted that a good activity should provide students with practice at appropriate difficulty levels. It should provide you with ways to support students by modeling strategies, guiding assignments, leading discussions, and even participating with them in word-play activities that are both fun *and* good instruction. We know that sometimes the best support comes from peers, so activities in which students can work in pairs or share their thoughts with others through discussion also provide excellent vocabulary practice.

As we noted, a good activity should also be authentic, providing practice with words in many different contexts. Such practice creates an awareness of the meaning and structure of words that will fascinate students and help make them lifelong word lovers.

In this chapter, we will peek in on some classroom activities where students and their teachers are learning new words—and learning about words—together!

Root of the Week

In Joanna Newton's second-grade classroom, words are everywhere. There are mathematics and social studies word walls as well as a student-created word wall that explores word families. One bulletin board of student writing has a banner that asserts, "Your Words Matter." Many of the students in Joanna's classroom have learned English as a second language. They speak a variety of first languages, including Spanish, Urdu, and Tupuri. She draws on their rich language backgrounds, often asking students to share words from their home cultures. In fact, her students start each day with a greeting in one of the home languages of a classmate.

Joanna says her students think prefixes, bases, and suffixes are "the greatest thing on earth." She shares that one day, a student joyfully observed that he loved "rocking with roots." The phrase caught on, and that is what her class now calls word study. So while some teachers may think that Greek and Latin word roots are too hard for primary-grade students, Joanna knows better.

Each Monday morning, she introduces her second graders to a new word root. After a short discussion about the root, she tapes a sheet of chart paper to a counter, writes the root at the top, and places a bowl of markers next to it. Her students spend the next few days on the lookout for words that contain the root.

They know that words from the root can appear when they read, listen, or talk to one another. They have also learned how to search for new words in dictionaries and on the internet. Each time they discover a word that fits, Joanna's students write it on the chart paper, always initialing the entry. On Friday mornings, her class assembles to review the collected words. Each student explains where they found the word, what it means, and how the root "gives you a clue." Classmates listen carefully to these explanations because they must decide whether the word is "real" or whether they need more information to confirm.

Root Word of the Day

Laura Hixenbaugh teaches fifth graders in an urban setting. For her students, vocabulary instruction has always meant memorizing spelling and definition lists, so a roots approach was unfamiliar to them. As she observes, "students weren't *thinking* about the words and word parts. They didn't expect to be asked to think. They were used to memorizing." When she began teaching word roots, she realized that the

first—and maybe most important—step in this process might be to build students' awareness of root words in their own familiar environment.

Every week, Laura and her students focus on one new root. Each day of the week, she selects a different word containing that root—one she thinks is particularly interesting or useful. This becomes the Word of the Day. Laura challenges students to use the Word of the Day as often as possible; she does this too. Each time students hear or see the word, they raise two fingers in a V. In Laura's class, the V stands for "Vocabulary." Laura reports that students love this activity and that it appears to have heightened their awareness of words.

Did You Know?

Activities such as Root of the Week and Root of the Day help students become "word aware." These activities can be used even in the earliest of grades by asking students to be on the lookout for the word family of the day or week!

There are many effective classroom approaches to Word of the Day, but we think Laura's is perfect for root study because the daily word provides an authentic semantic and linguistic context for the root. It also encourages her students to become both active listeners and articulate communicators. When they hear or use the daily word in a variety of real-life situations, students quickly come to understand that the same word can be used in many different ways. One week, for example, students are studying the root *port*, which means "carry." On Tuesday, the daily word is *report*. One of Laura's first jobs each day is to *report* the lunch count to the office. Laura mentions that *report* cards will be coming out soon and reminds students to get their social studies *reports* in by Friday. On that day, students have heard and used *report* as a verb, an adjective, and a noun. Although the word's meaning is somewhat different in each form, they now understand that even in its many different forms, the word *report* still contains the basic meaning of "carrying" information. This is why we agree with Laura when she says the daily word helps her students to think about words and word parts.

"Root of the Week" (Newton, Padak, and Rasinski 2008) or "Root Word of the Day" are both quick and easy ways to focus attention on words that share a prefix or a root word. Just post a chart with the root at the top. Number each line. Tell students that whenever they discover a word with that root, they should add it to the list. Tell them to write the word, circle the word part, and write where the word was found. At the end of the day or week, review the list. Students love hunting for these words, so you may find your class filling more than one sheet a week. Find a spot in the room to collect all the charts. As the days and weeks pass, you will have many lists of words that can be used for different purposes.

Roots around the School

Kelly Lochner, a middle school reading coach, noticed almost immediately the impact that a regular roots approach to vocabulary instruction had on students in her school. "We began by introducing a new root each week throughout the school. I provided leadership to the staff on how to approach roots with students. I asked the ELA teachers to introduce the new root and its meaning at the beginning of each week and spend no more than 10 minutes brainstorming a set of words that belonged to the root family. I asked the teachers to discuss with students how the meaning of each word was related to the root." Throughout each week, the ELA teacher would find ways to draw students' attention back to the root and related words. Other teachers in the school were also asked to find ways to bring the root of the week into their own instruction, even if for only a minute.

"It wasn't difficult for the science, mathematics, and social studies teachers to make connections with the week's root and their subject areas," Kelly says. "So many of the words in these content areas are based on the roots we were studying in English. The key was to help students see how the root and the words belonging to the root family crossed into many subject areas."

Kelly notes that the teaching of roots has helped all students with reading comprehension but has been especially helpful for her struggling readers. "Recognizing and knowing how to apply root meanings is especially valuable for my students whose vocabularies are not as broad as I would like them to be," she says. "Often, these students will encounter words in their reading that initially seem unsolvable. They used to freeze or just say the first few sounds and make something up. If students can recognize the meaning of just one part, usually a root, of a difficult word, this provides them a toehold on those previously unsolvable words. They do not give up as easily because they have knowledge they can use to conquer the word."

Realia and Children's Literature

Teachers Gwen Kraeff and Sharon Milligan use primary sources, real-world artifacts (realia), and children's literature to help their students build background knowledge for a new root. Realia are often used to heighten interest, build conceptual understanding, or activate background knowledge to support students when they read a difficult text (Rasinski, Padak, and Fawcett 2010). In the following example, Gwen and Sharon use realia to support students as they learn *graph/gram* ("write, draw"). This is an important root that appears in many abstract or conceptually difficult content-area words, including *graph*, *telegraph*, *telegram*, *seismograph*, *cardiogram*, *polygraph*, *lithograph*, and *sonogram*.

To introduce *graph/gram*, Gwen and Sharon first pass around realia of *graph/gram* words they brought in to share with their students: a *photograph* of Sharon's son; a *biography* of *Snowflake Bentley* (Martin 1998); and images of a *telegram*, *cardiogram*, and *hologram* they found online and printed. Sharon asks students to identify each item. As they respond, Gwen lists each word on the board. Sharon notes that occasionally this step may need scaffolding. For example, "If they say the photograph is a 'picture,' I help them come up with the word *photograph*." When each word is added, students are told to "discuss with your neighbor what you think the word means." When the list is finished, students are asked to figure out what all the words have in common. Students quickly notice that each word contains *graph* or *gram*, so Sharon asks them to "guess what they think *graph/gram* means."

After confirming that *graph/gram* means "write" or "draw," Gwen and Sharon tell students that *Snowflake Bentley* is a *biography* about a man who "*photographs* snowflakes." They read the fascinating tale of the "boy who loved snow" to their class, pointing out specific pages they have marked in the book that help define the word *photograph*.

This lesson gives students a chance to see concrete examples of some of the words generated by a root they are studying. We have noticed that as students become familiar with a concept, they may also bring things in to add to the teacher's realia, creating a mini-museum that everyone can enjoy (Rasinski, Padak, and Fawcett 2010). In following the activity with a read-aloud, Gwen and Sharon enhance their students' experience by combining word study and social studies. By choosing read-aloud books around the root being studied in a content area they are already learning, students experience repeated exposure—thereby creating a general familiarity with the root in an enjoyable way (Wexler 2019).

Of course, no matter the topic, listening to stories is always one of the best ways to heighten interest and deepen conceptual knowledge for students of all ages. Happily, there are countless texts that can support your study of roots. Like Gwen and Sharon, you can look for texts that will scaffold conceptual knowledge about a particular root, or just share lighthearted stories, such as *Max's Words* (Banks 2006) or *The Boy Who Loved Words* (Schotter 2006). Texts such as these reveal the power of words through the adventures of young characters with whom your students will easily identify. Remember to include texts that feature word play. Even if Amelia Bedelia's word mishaps in *Amelia Bedelia's Treasury* (Parish 1995) or *Mom and Dad Are Palindromes* (Shulman 2006) do not directly teach roots, they do teach students about the nature of words—an important goal of word study.

Writing an *Exciting* Story

Lara Shiplett has developed this third-grade writing activity so that her students can practice the new words they have learned with the prefix *ex–* by using them in what she calls a "creative and meaningful way." She begins by sharing an *"Exciting Story"* she has written on the board. First, she reads it to them, and then the whole class reads it together:

> With lights flashing and sirens blaring, the fire engine exited the firehouse quickly. The firefighters put on their fire equipment, including their breathing masks. They need to be sure to have their masks on so they can inhale and exhale safely.
>
> When they got to the burning house, one of the firefighters took a tall ladder and extended it up the exterior of the home.
>
> "My dog is still in the house!" a man exclaimed. Hearing the man, a firefighter rushed into the burning house and found the dog. The dog was very excited to be returned to his owner safe and unharmed.
>
> The excellence of the fire department was exhibited when the fire was extinguished. The homeowner was excited to be safe with his dog. The firefighters were exhausted!
>
> "Thank you, firefighters, for your excellent effort!" the man exclaimed.

As students pick out and discuss the different *ex–* words, Lara writes each one on chart paper. The class talks about her story, and she makes sure to emphasize how much she enjoyed using her imagination to come up with interesting ways to use the *ex–* words that they had learned that week. Then, Lara tells them it is their turn to use their imagination by selecting seven words from the chart and using them to write their own stories. She tells them that all their stories will be shared and enjoyed.

When the stories are finished, students are invited to read their selections in a "read-around." Lara reviews the rules of a read-around: whenever one person finishes, anyone can jump in and read their story until all the stories have been shared. She reminds her students that they cannot comment on any of the stories until all of them have been read. She also tells them to listen especially hard for the *ex–* words in order to see how many different ways the class has used them in the stories. After everyone has read, Lara makes sure that students talk about the various stories that were created and notice the different ways the *ex–* words were used. The students' stories are then displayed so that they can be read and enjoyed again and again.

In this activity, Lara has tailored a popular vocabulary strategy called Story Impressions (Blachowicz and Fisher 2015) to the study of roots. Story Impressions is a reading strategy in which the teacher lists several key words from a story in the order in which they appear. Students are then asked to write stories using the words in that order. When the stories are finished, students read them orally. Then, everyone reads the assigned text. In Lara's version, the words come from the same root, and students can use them in any order they choose.

Authors and Illustrators (Rasinski et al. 2019) is another variation that works well with root study. In this version, student pairs write stories. Once they have finished their stories, pairs trade stories with another student pair. Each team reads the new story and draws a picture to illustrate some part of it. Students then share illustrations, explaining what they drew and why they chose that part. You can tweak Authors and Illustrators for root study by inviting each team of students to brainstorm its own list of words using the root. You can also stipulate that students draw one of the root words as part of their illustrations. A discussion of their drawings is also a nice way to practice new vocabulary.

Words We Are Curious About

In Chapter 6, we described a practice activity called Words We Are Curious About. Emily Ulrich's fourth-grade students became so word curious that her Words We Are Curious About chart was always full. During a Graffiti Wall discussion about the root *trans–* ("across, change"), a student asked about the term *trans fat*. She wondered whether the term contained the root *trans–* or whether it was an example of a false etymology. Emily opened the question to her students, asking them to think about whether the word contained the root. Ultimately, the students were unsure. Emily admitted to the class that she was also unsure but was curious to know, modeling her own curiosity about words. She invited the student to add the word to the chart, stating that anyone who was interested was welcome to do some research and share back with the class. The research question was "Do *trans fats* have anything to do with 'changing' or going 'across'?"

trans fat

Is that the prefix *trans–* meaning "across, change"?

The next morning, three of Emily's students approached her, explaining that they had researched the word. One student used the internet for research at home, one asked her mother about the word, and one looked the word up in the glossary of a science text. All three had discovered that the word *trans fat* did in fact include the prefix *trans–*. At the end of their morning meeting, Emily invited the students to share what they learned about the word with the class and the processes they had used to research it: *trans fats* are fats that have been "changed" from liquid to solid form.

In total, Emily spent about 10 minutes of instructional time across two days. During these 10 minutes, Emily's students learned to use their knowledge of roots to think about and analyze a difficult academic term. They also learned about three different ways to independently figure out word meanings. Perhaps most importantly, they demonstrated word consciousness, that awareness of and interest in words that sparks motivation to learn about language.

Veni, Vidi, Vici

Rick Newton, one of the book's authors, studied Latin in school, but it was a "divide and conquer" word competition with homemade flash cards that truly fostered his love of English words. Every week on "Roots Day," his ninth-grade Latin teacher, Miss Cassell, passed out index cards and scissors and asked students to make their own flash cards for Latin prefixes, suffixes, and bases. Then, they competed with one another, sometimes in teams and sometimes individually, to see who could generate the greatest number of English words from a single Latin root:

> Even Miss Cassell got into the game. She created columns of words and followed each word with as many blanks as Latin roots it contained. We had to "slash" each word to identify the Latin roots and then deduce the definition. *Quadruped* had two blanks after it, so we whipped out our flash cards for *quadru* and *ped* and filled in the blanks with "four" and "foot." *Dissect* had two blanks: we filled in "cut" and "apart." *Compose* had two blanks: we filled in "put" and "together." We earned points that we could claim for extra credit toward our final grades in the course. This was serious fun!

By the end of the year, Rick and Miss Cassell's other students had become highly trained etymological dynamos. After all, there are only around 30 Latin prefixes, and they abound throughout our English vocabulary. Every Latin base they learned could generate at least 5—and often 15 or 20—English words. From *greg* (meaning "flock, group"), they formed *congregation, aggregate, gregarious, egregious, segregate,* and *desegregate.* And these were not just "dictionary words." These words appeared over and over in every course they took throughout high school and into college: words such as *perturb, revoke, providential, impediment,* and *implement.* The same words showed up on the ACT and SAT. Rick still remembers encountering *vivisect* on the SAT. He had never seen it before but was able to hazard an informed guess that it had something to do with "cutting" something "alive."

Miss Cassell's students learned the slogan "divide and conquer" when they read Julius Caesar in the ninth grade. But Miss Cassell taught them to "divide and conquer" vocabulary by showing them how to search for meaningful semantic units within unfamiliar, even intimidating, words. Miss Cassell's students reached a point where Julius Caesar's famous quote "*Veni, vidi, vici*" ("I came, I saw, I conquered") applied to their own approach to attacking and learning new words.

"Roots Day" is really just a variation of the popular word-study activity called Making and Writing Words (Rasinski 2001), in which students manipulate letter cards to make new words. In this version, students manipulate root cards to build new words. As they flip through their flash cards to build or analyze words, roots and meanings are naturally reinforced. And because this activity can easily be done in pairs or in competitive teams, students get a chance to talk about the words they are building.

Cognate Connections

In Chapter 2, we introduced an essential feature of root study, the concept of *cognates*, or root families: words containing the same root have a shared meaning. We noted that cognates enable us to draw meaningful connections between words we know or that are conceptually easy and words that are either unknown or more difficult to grasp. In fact, when students learn how to use cognates to figure out the meaning of new words, they have a "root awakening" that will serve them for the rest of their lives.

We began this chapter by peeking in on Joanna Newton's second-grade classroom. We end by taking a final look at a root awakening shared by two of her students, Maria and Arturo, in a guided-reading group.

Maria and Arturo are both English learners. Maria was born in El Salvador, and Arturo was born in Guatemala; they share Spanish as a home language. One morning, Joanna was preparing their group to read a nonfiction book called *The Romans*, part of the *Footsteps* series published by Franklin Watts, which provides an introductory tour for young readers of life in ancient Rome. Joanna asked the students to walk through the text, look at the pictures, and write three "wonder" questions they had about the ancient Romans that they thought might be answered in the book. The students then shared their wonder questions with each other.

Aqueduct was a key word in the text, and Joanna knew that it would be a new concept for her students. She also knew it was a perfect word for root study. She wrote *aqueduct* on the board, putting a rectangle around the root *duct*.

aque|duct|

Joanna told the group that *duct* means "lead." Then, she asked Maria whether she could use the root *duct* to predict what an aqueduct might be. Arturo immediately broke into a smile. While Maria focused intently on *duct*, he kept pointing to the first part of the word. As soon as Arturo blurted out, "agua, agua," Maria broke into a smile and said "water." Arturo explained how he knew "agua" and "aque" must mean the same thing, because he knew many Spanish words came from Latin roots. The group then considered both roots. If *agua* and *aque* both meant "water" and *duct* meant "lead," an *aqueduct* must be something that "leads" "water." They located a picture of an aqueduct in the text. Joanna told them to read the text to find out how an aqueduct works. She also reminded them to be on the lookout for answers to their wonder questions.

We think this is a perfect example of how a roots approach empowers students. Maria and Arturo began the lesson with the understanding that word parts have meaning. Moreover, they knew that many word parts have come to English from other languages. Arturo's understanding that he can figure out the meaning of a word by looking for cognates in all its word parts leads to an organic classroom discussion. And because Maria and Arturo bring the rich experience of another language to their English word study, these students have a deep linguistic background to draw upon. This "teachable moment" epitomizes our goal of word study: students working together as word sleuths, asking questions about meaning, and then trying to answer those questions by applying their knowledge of roots and cognates.

SUMMARY

In the last chapter, we outlined engaging classroom-tested activities for vocabulary practice. In this chapter, we shared teacher-tested examples of vocabulary activities as they unfolded in real classroom settings. Even though these vignettes highlight specific levels, all of them can be adapted to any grade level. Because they are all student centered, these activities can provide your students with practice at appropriate difficulty levels. Some of these activities build background knowledge, some scaffold difficult concepts, and some provide opportunities for students to hear, read, write, and share. All demonstrate how teachers and students can work together in ways that help students make connections between the new words they are learning and the ones they already know. In the next chapter, we will provide additional linguistic and teaching tips that may be helpful in supporting your students.

CHAPTER 8

More Strategies for Building Words

Language is a living entity that we use every day in spoken and written forms. As we use it, we create new words to fit new discoveries. We also expand the meaning of familiar words to fit new situations. Over 1,500 years old, the English language has survived and thrived in large part because it is so highly adaptable. Depending on its context, a single word can carry more than a single meaning. Words, then, are *flexible* in the ways we use them. Yet as teachers, we often encourage students to find the one "correct answer." This approach is not effective in teaching vocabulary because it creates a mindset that is at odds with the nature of words themselves.

Students with a good vocabulary tend to be interested in words and in the stories behind them. Assigning word lists and formal definitions will not give our students the skills or confidence to engage successfully with academic vocabulary. Instead, vocabulary instruction should stress *flexibility* (the Latin base *flect, flex* means "bend," the opposite of "rigid"). When students study roots, they learn how to *flex* with words, and they learn how to *reflect* on a word's history and meaning. This is what we aim to foster. In this chapter, we talk about *flexing* with words and *reflecting* on their meanings and forms. We explain how to "divide and conquer" words according to their bases, and we give some tips on how to *flex* roots into definitions that make sense.

Flexing the Meaning

So, what do we actually mean by the term *flexing*? Let us take a deeper look at the Latin base *flect, flex*. With its core meaning of "bend," *flexible* can describe the literal, physical characteristics of a rubber band. When our bodies are *flexible*, we can easily bend and physically touch our toes. But *flexible* does not always refer to literal bending; our schedules can be *flexible*, and teachers can follow *flexible* rules in the classroom without moving a muscle. While a basic sense of "bend" still applies in these contexts, the meaning has shifted from *literal* to *figurative*. The basic idea of "bending," though straightforward, is applicable to many situations. A *flexible* schedule cannot be physically bent, but it can be "modified, adjusted, altered, adapted."

The word *reflect* displays similar characteristics. We see our *reflection* in the mirror as a result of the literal and physical "bending" "back" (Latin prefix *re–* = "back, again") of light rays when they hit *reflective* glass. *Reflection* is an everyday word that we hear and use in school and at home. In physics, we learn about "the angle of incidence" and the "angle of *reflection*." *Reflection* is a technical word from science. But we can also engage in *reflection* about our teaching; we aspire to be *reflective* teachers. When we *reflect* on something, we view it with our mind's eye from different angles, and no *reflective* surfaces are required! Light colors are literally *reflective* of heat, but we ponder and meditate when we are in a figuratively *reflective* mood. A single word can have more than a single meaning. Vocabulary is anything but rigid.

For these reasons, students need to understand two important aspects of language before they can become effective word sleuths:

- The same word can have multiple meanings, depending on the context in which it is used. This feature is called *polysemy*, a Greek-based term meaning "multiplicity of meaning" (*poly–* = "many"; *sem* = "mean," "indicate").

- Words can have both a literal and a figurative meaning. The semantic range of a base, despite its simple meaning, is often wide and flexible.

Flexing the Form

Of equal importance with the two *semantic* aspects of a word is a third aspect that deals with its *form*. We have pointed out that the meaning of a word evolves over time. So too does its form. Like most Latin bases, *flect, flex* has two forms; some bases have three or even four. Fortunately, the various forms of a single base often look alike and are easily learned together (e.g., *duc, duct* = "lead"; *vid, vis*= "see"; *audi, audit* = "hear"; *trac, tract* = "pull, drag, draw"; *mov, mot, mobil* = "move"). Students benefit enormously from learning all forms of a base at the same time, since these forms are often preceded by prefixes and followed by suffixes.

A suffix is especially useful in *flexing* words because it can change the function (i.e., part of speech) and thereby the meaning of a word. In fact, when students start putting the pieces together, they are often amazed at how many words they can generate from a single base. Here is a partial list of some "bending" words that are related to one another. In their parts of speech, these words range from nouns and adjectives to verbs and adverbs:

- *flex* (verb), *flexible* (adjective), *flexibility* (noun), *flexor* (noun)

- *inflexible* (adjective), *inflexibility* (noun), *inflexibly* (adverb)

- *reflex* (noun), *reflexive* (adjective)

- *reflect* (verb), *reflective* (adjective), *reflection* (noun)

- *deflect* (verb), *deflection* (noun), *deflective* (adjective)

- *inflect* (verb), *inflection* (noun), *inflectional* (adjective)

Taken together, a heightened awareness of these three aspects of language makes students *flexible* and *reflective* builders of vocabulary. When students *flex* word parts and see how many connections they can make between words, their interest grows.

A "Spectacular" Etymology

Every word has a history based on the meaning of its roots. A word's history is its *etymology*, a Greek-based term meaning the "study of true meaning" (*etym* = "true, truth"; *–ology* = "study of"). The true meaning of almost every academic vocabulary word is to be found in its etymology. Happily, a word's etymology almost always has an interesting story behind it. Let's take a look at some *spectacular* words from the Latin base *spect, spic*, which means "watch, look at." We begin with this "Did You Know?" from Level 4 of the *Building Vocabulary from Word Roots* curriculum.

SPECTACLES: THEN AND NOW

The word *spectacle* comes from the Roman tradition of public games and circuses. To win popularity, Roman politicians put on elaborate shows for all the people. These events were free of charge and drew enormous crowds of *spectators* who flocked to watch *spectacles* of animals and gladiators fighting one another. Politicians would compete with one another by producing more and more elaborate games. They aimed to make their shows more *spectacular* than all the others. Eventually, the Romans built the enormous Colosseum to hold the crowds of onlookers. Even today, we talk about showy things that we remember as *spectacular*. Have you ever seen a *spectacular* fireworks display on the Fourth of July? These events are often sponsored by local officials and remind us of the *spectacles* of Roman times.

Notice the flexible forms of the "watch, look at" base and its suffixes in this passage: *spectacle(s)*, *spectacular*, *spectators*. Now, notice that all these words have a clear connection with "watching, looking at" things that attract attention. To this day, we associate *spectator* sports with crowds and large stadiums. We still say, "Do not make a *spectacle* of yourself" to someone who is "making a scene" and attracting onlookers.

Think about how the original meaning of *spectacle* ("a game or entertainment looked at by crowds") has expanded over time. When eyeglasses were invented in the 13th century, they were called *spectacles*. This makes sense: *spectacles* enable us to "look at" things with clarity. But this new use of the word comes with a *flexed* sense: as eyeglasses, *spectacles* are what we use to see *with*. We do not look *at* spectacles, we look *through* them. This new meaning stands side by side with the original meaning of the eye-catching games that the Romans watched. *Spectacles* are *spectacular* shows as well as eyeglasses. Because language is in constant use and because contexts are always changing, the meaning of *spectacles* has become quite flexible. But the base meaning of "watch, look at" persists.

In the 18th century, some five hundred years after the invention of *spectacle*s, Benjamin Franklin came up with a lens that had two focal points, one for distance and one for close-up vision. He named his invention *double spectacles* (over time, this term was changed to *bifocals*). Think for a moment about how hilarious this phrase would have sounded to the ancient Romans: a *double spectacle* would have sounded to them like a double feature at the movie theater or a doubleheader at a ballpark would sound to

us today. Gladiators *and* acrobats on the same day! A double spectacle! The ancient Romans did not have eyeglasses, but they gave us the roots for the modern-day words we use to describe them. Roots even allow us to pun, as in this groan-worthy riddle: Question: "What do you say to someone who is turning into a pair of glasses?" Answer: "Stop making a *spectacle* of yourself!"

This short history of the word *spectacle* is the sort of thing that students enjoy and remember. When they learn how to be reflective about vocabulary, students also develop "word curiosity." They come to understand that word meanings are not random. Best of all, as they look for connections between words, they are engaged and active learners—not passive memorizers of definitions.

Flexing and Reflecting with *Spect, Spic*

Next, let us reflect on some other *spect, spic* words, staying *flexible* and alert to three key aspects of language (multiple meanings/polysemy; literal and figurative meanings; suffixes):

> ### Did You Know?
> The ancient Romans did not have eyeglasses, but they gave us the roots for the modern-day words we use to describe them. Roots even allow us to pun, as in this groan-worthy riddle: Question: "What do you say to someone who is turning into a pair of glasses?" Answer: "Stop making a *spectacle* of yourself!"

- An *inspector* literally "looks" "into" things and conducts an *inspection* (*in–* = "in, on, into").

- An artist literally "looks" "through" a far distance to depict *perspective* in a painting (*per–* = "through"). But our *perspective* can also be our point of view, the way we "look at" something figuratively, with our mind's eye.

- When we are *introspective* and engage in *introspection*, we take a figurative "look" "inside" ourselves and examine our thoughts (*intro–* = "inside"). Even with our eyes shut, we can be *introspective* and take an "inside look."

- When we are *retrospective*, we figuratively "look" "behind, backward" and reconsider past events (*retro–* = "backward, behind"). In *retrospect*, we may regret something we said or did. *Retrospection* is hindsight—of the figurative kind.

- During the 1800s Gold Rush in American history, *prospectors* were literally "looking" "ahead" as they made their way to California for gold (*pro–* = "forward, ahead"). They kept a "watch" for metallic flecks in streams and *prospected* in the sand of riverbeds.

- At the beginning of a course of study, a teacher may hand out a *prospectus*, an outline that figuratively "looks" "ahead" to the topics to be covered. A school may prepare for its *prospective* students by figuratively "looking" "ahead" to the time that children in the district will reach school age. When we choose a course of study for college, we consider the *prospects* of a career by figuratively "looking" "ahead" to the future.

- *Suspects* are kept "under" "watch" for *suspicious* behavior (observe the two forms of the base, *spect, spic*) (*sus–, sub–* = "under, below, up from under"). Sneaky characters are *suspicious* (= "untrustworthy"). But we are also *suspicious* (= "untrusting") of sneaky characters. We *suspect* them of being up to no good and figuratively keep them under our eye.

- When something is *conspicuous*, it stands out and draws the attention of many onlookers (*con–* = "very"; an intensifying prefix). *Conspicuous* consumers are show-offs who try to get a lot of people to "look" at them.

- When we are *expecting* a package, we stay on the "look" "out" (*ex–* = "out") for the delivery truck. But a mother-to-be can also be *expecting*, or "looking" "out" for, her baby to arrive. (**Note:** Because the prefix *ex–* is pronounced with a final /s/ sound as part of the *x*, the base *spect* is spelled without initial *s*. We do not write "exspect." Stay flexible!)

These are just some of the over one hundred words based on *spect, spic* that students will encounter from kindergarten through high school. We cannot, and thankfully need not, teach each and every derivative, and we certainly should not teach a dizzying list of definitions. This is not the goal of the roots approach. Instead, our goal is to instill word curiosity and encourage students to look for meaningful connections between words they may have never thought about before. Once they have a root awakening, light bulbs start going off in their heads, and a "wow factor" erupts that makes vocabulary *spectacularly* fascinating!

Word Composition: Start with the Base

Just as the basement of a house provides an essential foundation for the entire structure, the base provides the entire word with its underlying meaning. In addition, just as a basement supports multiple stories and add-ons, the base of a word can add prefixes and suffixes to build a vast number of words. But no matter where it appears, the base is *always* the core of the word. This is why "bases are basic" is the motto of the *Building Vocabulary* curriculum.

As beginning readers, students learn to tackle a new word by moving from its first letter to its last. They soon learn to apply this left-to-right movement as they look for word-family letter patterns that generate the same sound. But these strategies do not work with most academic vocabulary. If students try to understand a new word by moving from left

to right, they will often produce explanations that make no sense. This is because a base is often preceded by a prefix.

Let us assume, for example, that the root of the week is *tract* = "pull, drag, draw" and that students are working with the word *contract*. Most students will quickly divide the word at the right spot: con/tract. They may already know that *con–* means "with, together." If they combine these parts in order of appearance (as they first learned to read), the resulting definition may come out as "with pull" or "together drag," neither of which makes sense.

This is why we ask students to "slash off" the prefix, identify the base, and then use its meaning as the first word of a definition. For the word *contract*, students first "divide and conquer" it by separating the prefix from the base: con/tract. Then, they identify the base *tract* as meaning "pull, drag, draw." To this core meaning, they add the meaning of the prefix. Students quickly catch on to this new skill since their revised definition of *contract* = "pull or draw together" makes sense. Moreover, once they have identified the basic meaning of *contract*, here are the multiple meanings (both literal and figurative) they now have access to:

- When muscles *contract*, they "draw" "together."

- When business partners sign a *contract*, they "draw" up legal papers "together."

- When writing the *contraction* "don't" instead of "do not," we "pull, draw" two short words "together" and mark this with an apostrophe.

When an etymology makes sense, students know they got it right! They may have an "aha" moment when they see that a *contraction* can describe a tense muscle and an abbreviated spelling. A "wow" factor comes from flexing.

Here is an analogy that may demonstrate why the base is of greater importance than the prefix. The Latin base *fix* means "fasten, attach." Business envelopes remind us to *affix* postage: we are to "fasten" a stamp "to" the letter (*ad–, af–* = "to, toward, add to"). But the letter must be there in the first place. The stamp is merely *affixed* to something essential. Nobody sends a lone stamp through the mail; the stamp's purpose is to get the letter to its recipient. Likewise, prefixes exist only as attachments, and the bases to which they attach provide

Did You Know?

Here is an analogy that may demonstrate why the base is of greater importance than the prefix. The Latin base *fix* means "fasten, attach." Business envelopes remind us to *affix* postage: we are to "fasten" a stamp "to" the letter (*ad–, af–* = "to, toward, add to"). But the letter must be there in the first place. The stamp is merely *affixed* to something essential. Nobody sends a lone stamp through the mail; the stamp's purpose is to get the letter to its recipient. Likewise, prefixes exist only as attachments, and the bases to which they attach provide the words' core meanings: bases are basic. Like postage stamps, prefixes serve no purpose in isolation. Similarly, prefixes are useful only when they attach to a base. A word, therefore, may often start with a prefix, and the prefix necessarily comes "before" the base (*pre–* = "before"), but the *meaning* of a word always begins with its base. We understand words from the inside out.

the words' core meanings: bases are basic. Like postage stamps, prefixes serve no purpose in isolation. Similarly, prefixes are useful only when they attach to a base. A word, therefore, may often start with a prefix, and the prefix necessarily comes "before" the base (*pre–* = "before"), but the *meaning* of a word always begins with its base. We understand words from the inside out.

Flexing and Reflecting with *Trac, Tract*

In Chapter 2, we learned that prefixes affect a word's meaning in three ways. They may negate, indicate direction, or intensify the force of the base. Most often, prefixes are directional (e.g., *under, down, with, apart, over*). Instead of requesting a formal definition, ask students to talk about the impact of the prefix on the base in determining the word's meaning. Guide students as they brainstorm and attach familiar prefixes to a base.

Below, you will find some examples of "pull, drag, draw" words built on *trac, tract*:

- A dentist who *extracts* a tooth "pulls" it "out." (*extract* = "pull out," not "out pull")

- Vanilla *extract* is the oily liquid "drawn" "out" of a vanilla bean. (not "out drawn")

- We feel "drawn to" *attractive* people. *Attractions* at amusement parks "draw" large crowds. (*attract* = "draw to, draw toward," not "toward draw")

- When we *subtract*, we "draw" one number in a column "from under" another. (*subtract* = "draw from under," not "under draw")

- A journalist may *retract* a statement and "withdraw" it by taking it "back." (*retract* = "pull back," not "back pull")

We can also generate words based on *trac, tract* that have no prefix:

- A *tractor* is a motorized vehicle that "pulls" farm equipment.

- When cars lose *traction* on icy roads, tires lose their "pull."

- When we *trace* a picture to make a "drawing," we "drag" our pencils across the paper and follow the lines. When we go "back" over lines we have just "drawn," we *retrace* them.

In all these examples, we see the benefits of flexing with the base meaning of "pull, drag, draw" in a variety of applications. A dentist literally "pulls" out a tooth by *extracting* it, but a journalist figuratively "draws" back an earlier statement with a *retraction*. In art class, we literally "draw" our pencils across the paper as we *trace*. But when we had to *retrace* our steps, we figuratively went back over our *tracks*. When muscles *contract*, they literally "draw" up and tighten, but when business partners "draw" up a *contract*, they figuratively "pull" together and make a deal.

As these examples demonstrate, the semantic range of a base, despite its essential simplicity, is often wide and flexible. Moreover, it can span both literal and figurative realms. Even though flexing word parts can be challenging at first, students quickly become fascinated by the many connections between words and ideas that they have never before seen as related.

The Ultimate Test: Does It Make Sense?

What if we have followed these steps and determined a meaning, but our definition does not make sense? If our understanding of a word is hazy or does not fit the context, we may have come up with a *false etymology*. If that happens, use a digital or a print dictionary to see whether you have identified the correct root meaning. Good dictionaries provide more than definitions. They can also give the word's roots, etymology, and usage over time. (See Appendix B.)

Let us look at the Latin base *terr*, which means "land, ground, earth." This base generates important words that students encounter in science and social studies:

- **terrain:** the land we walk or travel on; an expanse of earth, as smooth, steep, or rough

- **terrace:** a patio or a level surface that we can walk on like the ground itself

- **territory:** a tract of land that explorers investigate or that countries claim as property

- **terrarium:** a container for frogs, turtles, and plants that thrive on the ground or earth

- **extraterrestrial:** pertaining to outer space and regions "outside" the planet Earth (*extra–* = "outside") (Note: "Earth" refers to soil *and* the planet!)

Each of these *terr* words has a straightforward connection with "land, ground, earth." But did you know that the *Mediterranean Sea*, a body of water, also includes the base *terr*? What can the word *Mediterranean* have to do with "land"? The dictionary tells us that the word *Mediterranean* comes from the Latin bases *medi*, meaning "middle," and *terr*, meaning "land, ground, earth." It turns out that the *Mediterranean Sea* was named by the Romans because they believed it was the body of water that lay "in the middle of the lands" they ruled. In fact, the Romans believed that this sea was the "middle of the Earth." This etymological tidbit confirms that *Mediterranean* is indeed an "earth" word, and the definition now makes sense. This is the kind of word curiosity we want to encourage.

Now, let us move on to other *terr* words. The words *terrible, terror, terrorist, terrorism,* and *terrify* all look like "earth" words but have no apparent connection with the list we just examined. What do these words have in common? They all have something to do with "fear" and "fright." In fact, the dictionary tells us that these words come from the Latin base *terr(i)*, *terror*, meaning "fear, frighten." Any attempt to connect these look-alike "frightening" words with "earth" words would result in a false etymology because the same spelling/ sound patterns do not always have the same meaning. This is why students must learn to ask questions and look for answers when the meaning they have generated for a word does not make sense.

Furthermore, by questioning whether the *terr* in *terrify* has an "earth" connection, students have learned another base that will take them to more questions as they begin to think critically about words. For example, students may now ask about the *terrier* breed of dogs. How did these cute canines get that name? Are *terriers* connected to the "ground" or to "fear"? Did their high-pitched barking "frighten" people? This might be a reasonable first guess, but it does sound a bit forced. After all, other breeds of dogs that are not *terriers* are larger in size and more ferocious in their barks. But if *terriers* got their name because of something having to do with the "earth, ground," we may need to investigate. *Terriers* do, of course, walk on the "ground," but so do other dogs as well as human beings. What is so distinctive about them that they should have been given this name?

An etymological dictionary will answer our question. We learn that the word *terrier* was invented to describe these pets as "earth dogs," bred specifically to pursue and catch ground-burrowing animals, such as foxes, badgers, and chipmunks. The *terrier* and "earth" connection now makes sense! In the end, there is nothing "terrifying" about *terriers*. Another "aha" moment!

In the Classroom

To build vocabulary from word roots, therefore, we emphasize the base. We help students understand that the base always provides a word's core meaning. The overall process involves four steps:

1. Divide a word into its semantic parts ("divide and conquer" into prefix, base, suffix).

2. Identify the base to determine the word's core meaning.

3. Add the meaning of the prefix and/or the suffix after the base has been identified.

4. Check that the definition of the word makes sense in the context.

It is important to stress that the roots approach does not ask students to memorize each and every derivative of a base. Instead, we explore multiple derivatives, including words from daily situations (e.g., *tractor*, *trace*, *attractive*) and from academic contexts (e.g., *subtract*, *retraction*, *contraction*) to reinforce understanding of a newly learned base. The focus on building knowledge is the best strategy for preventing rote memorization, which, as research has proven time and again, does not work (Wexler 2019). As students begin to see connections between everyday words and the words they learn in school, their confidence soars.

In addition, this approach does not call for memorization of vocabulary lists and formal definitions. It calls, instead, for the memorization of word roots, which students "flex" into a deeper understanding of words they may already know. It also emboldens them to search for meaningful parts inside unfamiliar words they will encounter, particularly as they advance through grade levels and meet more challenging words. Word lists and dictionary definitions are soon forgotten. Word roots, by contrast, are hard to forget.

So, how might this approach work in the classroom? Let us go back to the root *terr* for a moment. We can introduce this base by asking student pairs to brainstorm *terr* words that refer to the "earth." As they share their lists, we should ask them to explain the "earth" connection in each word. Someone who loves dogs may offer *terrier* as a derivative, but you or another student might question the connection. Check the dictionary. Even better, ask your students to check the dictionary. As they share what they have found, everyone will experience the "wow" factor.

In the process, students have learned more than the meaning of a single word. They have learned how to find an answer to a question that they themselves raised as a result of being *reflective* about vocabulary. Our educational system conditions students to answer questions posed by teachers, who are expected to have all the "right answers" and who therefore might feel embarrassed to consult a dictionary in their presence. But that's OK—consulting the dictionary shows students that no one has all the answers and that the important thing is to be willing to look for them! Moreover, the roots approach conditions students to answer the question that *they* have raised. Anyone can easily forget the answer to a teacher's question, but we rarely forget the answer to a question that we ourselves have asked.

SUMMARY

This chapter has provided information and strategies that support a flexible approach to vocabulary instruction. While the core meaning of a word connects to its etymological roots, its meaning and form can change. For example, a single word often has multiple meanings, depending on its context. Moreover, those meanings can be either literal or figurative. For these reasons, students should not be required to memorize definitions from word lists. Rather, they should engage in exploring word roots (prefixes, bases, suffixes), which generate wide-ranging vocabulary from everyday and academic contexts. In the process, they will become curious about words and comfortable and confident with the process of flexing and reflection.

CHAPTER 9

Spelling Matters

Just as word meanings come with interesting histories, so do word spellings. For example, everyone knows the word *hiccup*. This curious word came into English in the 1600s to describe the sound we make when we take a sudden, short breath. This momentary spasm in breathing is spelled precisely as it sounds: *hiccup*. About one hundred years later, however, a new spelling emerged: *hiccough*. The new spelling became fashionable because most people thought it should be connected to meaning; they thought that a *hiccup* was a type of cough, and so they began writing it as *hiccough*. Although linguists consider the spelling *hiccough* to be a folk etymology (a popular but mistaken account of the origin of a word or a phrase), both spellings are acceptable in British and American usage. This is remarkable: most words ending in *ough* are pronounced with a final /f/ (*enough, rough, tough*) or long /o/ sound (*dough, although, thorough*). The word *hiccough*, however, is pronounced with a final /p/ sound, in violation of the rules. It appears that word spellings, like word meanings, can evolve over time. We pay attention to spelling because *spelling matters*!

Spelling is governed by rules that have many exceptions, which requires us to be *flexible* in the way we approach words. This chapter will give some tips to share with students about how their knowledge of roots can help them unlock not only the meaning of a word but also its spelling. Let's begin with a short summary of the three basic aspects of English words that support students' spelling development.

Spelling and Vocabulary Development: From Sound to Meaning

Understanding that word meanings are not just the result of a random stringing together of letters is a powerful discovery for students. Knowing that each new word they encounter has an internal logic and structure enables them to look inside unfamiliar words for recognizable parts and patterns. In the process, students can unlock the meaning of the academic vocabulary words they need to be successful in school. So what does this have to do with spelling?

Templeton and Morris (2000) believe that students draw on three kinds of information "cues" as they encounter new words: alphabetic, pattern, and meaning. These scholars have developed a model for helping us think about spelling development in a way that is linked to the kinds of vocabulary students encounter as they progress through school.

As noted earlier, emergent readers learn how to "sound out" words by matching letters and sounds in a left-to-right direction. They approach a word from beginning to end. For example, the word *cat* is made up of three distinct sounds /c/ /a/ /t/. Children encounter this word in a variety of settings and figure out that each letter of the alphabet represents a particular sound. As teachers, we know that the *–at* in the word *cat* is also a letter pattern that represents the sound /at/ in many words. For this reason, we give our students many opportunities to see the *–at* pattern in all kinds of words.

As children move through the primary grades, they learn letter patterns as word families. As patterns grow more complex, students begin to encounter words whose vowel sounds blend with consonants in different configurations. This is why in Levels K–2 of the *Building Vocabulary* curriculum, we use poems and activities to help students grasp the new complexity, from long- and short-vowel sound word families (CVCe: *flame, rake*) to diphthongs (*ou, ow*), digraphs (i.e., *igh*), and r-controlled vowels (*cart, fern, port*). As they encounter new words and internalize new patterns, students come to understand that spelling does not always work in a left-to-right direction. Instead, they need to look for letter patterns (often syllables) that consistently represent one sound: *flame* (*same, shame, tame*), *rake* (*lake, take, bake*), *right* (*night, fight, bright*). The list goes on and on!

From third grade on, however, most new words that students encounter exhibit a different letter pattern, one based on meaning. This is because students have moved to deeper study of the content areas: science, mathematics, social studies, and language arts. As we noted earlier, almost all content-area vocabulary words come from Greek and Latin. Moreover, as students continue through elementary, middle, and high school, they will encounter much of this vocabulary through reading. This is why Levels 3–11 of the *Building Vocabulary* curriculum use reading and writing activities to help students identify the meaning patterns in prefixes, suffixes, and bases. As they encounter the same root in new words, students come to recognize meaning from these patterns. For example, they begin to see a pattern in words such as *export, import, report, reporter, airport, transport,* and *transportation.* These words are not connected by sound alone. The *port* word family is also a word root—a root is a word part that carries meaning, and this particular root means "carry."

You can see why we often talk about vocabulary development as a movement from sound to meaning. Although early readers begin with word families that represent alphabetic sound patterns, most school vocabulary comes from word roots that represent semantic meaning patterns. Moreover, as *hiccup/hiccough* remind us, many new—often surprising and interesting—patterns can emerge that change how a word is spelled. In the rest of this chapter, we share tips from the *Building Vocabulary* curriculum for spelling words with prefixes, bases, and suffixes that will help your students learn common spelling patterns as they unlock the meanings of new words.

Spelling Tips for Latin-Based Vocabulary

In the following three subsections, we point out the spelling patterns that occur in the prefixes and suffixes of Latin-based vocabulary. We provide several useful tips that are based on these patterns.

PREFIX PATTERNS

The most common spelling error in English has to do with the doubling of a consonant. Is it spelled *effective* or *efective*? *Illegal* or *ilegal*? *Immigrant* or *imigrant*? *Oppose* or *opose*? *Aggravate* or *agravate*? *Difference* or *diference*? *Attractive* or *atractive*? Since we cannot hear the difference between a single and double consonant, the spelling seems random. There is, however, a pattern shared by all these words: each begins with a Latin prefix that ends with a consonant.

In many words, the prefix attaches to the base and creates no pronunciation or spelling confusion: we put the car in *reverse* to go "back" (*re–* = "back, again"); we *descend* the staircase when we go "down" (*de–* = "down, off"); we make *progress* when we move "ahead" (*pro–* = "ahead, forward, for"). Note that these prefixes (*re–, de–, pro–*) all end in vowels. When we pronounce vowels, our mouths are open, ready to pronounce the next letter. Prefixes that end in vowels, therefore, do not give rise to spelling confusion.

Sometimes, however, when a prefix meets a base, it undergoes a spelling change to make the word easier to pronounce. The final consonant of the prefix changes to match—or *assimilates* ("likens" itself "to") to—the first consonant of the base. The result is a doubled consonant near the beginning of the word. Although assimilation is a technical-sounding word, it is a simple and straightforward concept. Students simply need to know that prefixes sometimes change spelling to make words easier to pronounce.

In short, if a prefix ending in a consonant attaches to a base beginning with a consonant, the final consonant of the prefix may change to make the word easier to pronounce. This change is called *assimilation*.

Here is a list of the most frequently assimilated prefixes:

- *in–* (= "not") + legal = illegal (not *inlegal*)
- *in–* (= "in") + migrate = immigrate (not *inmigrate*)
- *con–* (= "with, together") + lect = collect (not *conlect*)
- *ad–* (= "to, toward, add to") + tract = attract (not *adtract*)
- *sub–* (= "under, below") + fer = suffer (not *subfer*)
- *ex–* (= "out") + fort = effort (not *exfort*)
- *ob–* (= "up against") + pose = oppose (not *obpose*)

You can spot an assimilated prefix when there is a double consonant near the beginning of a word. When students are alerted to this spelling pattern, they can quickly recognize the prefix and unlock the meaning while also learning the correct spelling. Here are examples of a few assimilated words from each prefix that ends in a consonant:

- *in–* becomes *im–, il–: immature, immerse; illiterate, illegible, illegitimate*
- *con–* becomes *com–, col–: community, communicate, commotion; collaborate, collision*
- *ad–* becomes *at–, ap–, as–, af–, ag–, ar–, ac–, an–: attractive, appear, assent, affection, aggravate, arrest, accelerate, announce*
- *sub–* becomes *sup–, suf–: suppose, support, sufficient*
- *ex–* becomes *ef–: effort, effect, efficient*
- *ob–* becomes *oc–, of–, op–: occur, offend, opposition*

Each word contains a doubled consonant near the beginning: the sign of an assimilated prefix!

What Students Need to Know about Assimilation

Our explanation of assimilation may provide more information than your students need in order to deal with prefixes and spelling. We present it here so that you, as the teacher, will understand the logic that drives many spelling and pronunciation changes in academic vocabulary. (For a deeper dive into assimilation, including detailed word lists and teaching tips, see Appendix E.) So, what *do* students need to know?

- Although they do not need to know all the prefixes and examples we share, it is helpful for students to see how cumbersome it is to say words such as *subport* and how easy it is to say assimilated words such as *support*. We want students to understand the reason behind assimilation—to make words easier to pronounce.

- Whenever a double consonant appears near the beginning of a word, students should divide the word between the doubled consonant. They should look for the base and then identify the altered prefix. This is where the strategy of "divide and conquer" is especially helpful.

SUFFIX PATTERNS

Prefixes are just one word part that can affect spelling. Suffixes can too. A suffix changes both the function (i.e., part of speech) and meaning of a word. Look at how the suffixes *–less*, *–y*, *–ful*, *–ly*, and *–ness* generate five new meanings for the word *taste*: *tasteless* (adjective = "without taste" or "lacking manners"); *tasty* (adjective = "flavorful"); *tasteful* (adjective = "stylish," "exhibiting good manners"); *tastefully* (adverb = "in a manner conforming to good taste"); *tastefulness* (noun = "the state of being tasteful"). Because the spelling of most suffixes remains stable across many base words, when students recognize the letter patterns, they readily grasp both meaning and spelling. The following are tips to share about a few commonly used suffixes:

- The suffix *–ful* does not affect the spelling of base words ending in *–e* (e.g., *care–careful*; *peace–peaceful*). The final *y* of a base word changes to *i* before this suffix is added (*beauty–beautiful*). The final *l* of a base word is retained, resulting in a double *l* near the end of the word (*careful–carefully*; *final–finally*).

- The suffix *–less* does not affect the spelling of base words ending in *–e* (*hope–hopeless*; *wire–wireless*). The final *y* of a base word changes to *i* before this suffix is added (*penny–penniless*).

- When the suffix *–ify* attaches to a base word ending in *y* or *e*, the final vowel is dropped (*pure–purify, false–falsify, simple–simplify, beauty–beautify, glory–glorify*). When words ending in *–ify* are inflected, the final *y* changes to *i* (*magnify–magnifies–magnified–magnifier; petrify–petrifies–petrified; unify– unifies–unified–unifier*).

- When determining which spelling of the suffix *–or, –er* to use: If the base word is a monosyllabic verb that stands by itself, the suffix is usually *–er* (*teach– teacher; paint–painter; read–reader; wait–waiter*). If the base word contains two or more syllables, the suffix is usually spelled *–or* (*instruct–instructor; contract–contractor; profess–professor*). Additionally, many verbs ending in the suffix *–ate* have corresponding nouns that indicate the people or things that "do" these activities. In most cases, these nouns end in *–or*, not *–er* (*educate– educator; illustrate–illustrator; investigate– investigator; operate–operator*).

IS IT *–IBLE* OR *–ABLE*? IS IT *–ANT* OR *–ENT*? LOOK FOR THE PATTERN!

When determining which spelling of *–ible* or *–able* to use, look for the pattern of other words built on the same base. If other words from the same base are spelled with an *i* immediately after the base, write the suffix *–ible*.

- *audible* (not "audable"): compare *audition, auditorium, audio*

- *credible* (not "credable"): compare *credit, creditor*

- *visible* (not "visable"): compare *vision, visit*

- *digestible* (not "digestable"): compare *digestion*

If other words from the same base are spelled with an *a* immediately after the base, write the suffix *–able*.

- *portable* (not "portible"): compare *transportation, importation, deportation*

- *habitable* (not "habitible"): compare *habitat, habitation, inhabitant*

- *operable* (not "operible"): compare *operate, operation*

If an adjective ends in *–ant*, its corresponding noun is spelled as *–ance* or *–ancy* (never as *–ence, –ency!*): *important–importance; abundant–abundance; vacant–vacancy*.

If an adjective ends in *–ent*, its corresponding noun is spelled as *–ence* or *–ency* (never as *–ance, –ancy!*): *obedient–obedience; independent– independence; urgent–urgency*.

Spelling Tips for Greek-Based Vocabulary

Greek-based vocabulary poses spelling challenges of a different sort. First, the words tend to be long. As a word grows in length, so does the likelihood that a misspelling will occur. Second, Greek-based words are encountered in specialized contexts. Unlike most Latin-based vocabulary, which displays extremely high frequency, Greek-based words have limited and less frequent application. Words such as *philosophy*, *geometric*, *polygon*, *photosynthesis*, and *archaeological* not only sound Greek but also refer to highly academic matters. A student's ability to comprehend an entire passage in a textbook dealing with mathematics, science, technology, social studies, or language arts often hinges on a single Greek-based word. Shakespeare's famous quote, "It was Greek to me!" plays on this notion of Greek as a specialized language for the educated.

Fortunately, Greek-based words display spelling patterns that are consistent and reliable. These patterns become especially apparent when we sound out the words with our students. Use these spelling tips for Greek-based vocabulary:

- Most Greek-based words are pronounced exactly as they are spelled: every vowel is sounded out. The name *Socrates* (SAW-kruh-teez) is trisyllabic and does not rhyme with *crates*!

- With the exception of the initial "silent *p*" in words such as *pseudonym* and *psychology*, every letter, or digraph, in a Greek-based word is pronounced and spelled just as it sounds: *hematology*, *polytheism*, *anesthesia*. When students sound out the syllables, the spelling follows most of the rules they learned as beginning readers.

- The plural form of Greek-based words ending in *–sis* is spelled *–ses*, pronounced with a long *e* (rhymes with "sees"): *thesis-theses*, *analysis-analyses*.

- The sound /f/ in Greek-based words is almost always spelled as *ph*: *photography*, *philosopher*, *physical*, *phantom*, *phenomenon*, *phobia*. The presence of *ph* in a word is often a sign that it is Greek based.

- The combined letters *ch* in Greek-based words are pronounced as /k/: *character*, *choral*, *choreography*, *chemistry*, *Achilles*, *ichthyology*, *chronology*, *schism*. The presence of a hard *ch* in a word is often a sign that it is Greek based.

- Unlike Latin-based words, many Greek words contain an internal *y* that is pronounced like a short /i/. This is especially common in words with the Greek prefix *syn–*, *sym–* ("with, together"): *synthesis*, *sympathy*, *symphony*, *synchronize*, *synonym*. Other examples include *cyclical*, *physics*, *chlorophyll*, and *analysis*.

- In long words, Greek roots are often joined together by a connecting *o*. Students should "divide and conquer" these words at the juncture points where the "connecting *o*" appears: *electr/o/cardi/o/gram*, *phot/o/synthesis*, *acr/o/phobia*, *klept/o/mania*, *therm/o/dynamic*, *orth/o/graphic*, *hier/o/glyphics*.

A Word about Greek and Latin Bases

Just as prefixes and suffixes display patterns that help us with spelling, the bases of academic vocabulary words likewise contain some built-in spelling pointers. In borrowing bases from Greek and Latin, English has simplified many complexities.

WHY DO SOME BASES HAVE MULTIPLE FORMS?

The English language, with its long and fascinating history, has incorporated word roots from many different languages. In the process, it has removed many of the intricate details that characterize the original tongues. For example, the original Latin verb (in its four principal parts) *moveo, movere, movi, motus* means "move." The participle, *motus, mota, motum*, means "having been moved." The adjective *mobilis, mobile* means "able to be moved, mobile." But English has distilled these multiple forms into three simple variations: all English words dealing with "movement" are based on *mov, mot, mobil*. It's as simple as that! These three forms, all sharing the foundation of *mo*, are easily recognized as being related. Such words as *movement, remove, motion, promotion, commotion, motivate*, and *mobility* are all cognates. They were all born together from a common root. Students of English need not bother with declensions and conjugations; they need only to associate the basic concept of "movement" with all *mov, mot, mobil* words. Bases are basic—in more ways than one!

By contrast, a typical Latin verb has four distinct "principal parts," which can be inflected into well over three hundred different forms. These forms express changes in tense, voice, mood, number, gender, and part of speech. A typical Greek verb has six principal parts that can be inflected into over four hundred forms. Students of ancient languages must learn a myriad of different spellings! Happily, students of English need to memorize just a few forms for each root. Most Latin bases exhibit two forms, and a few have three or four. Most Greek bases have just one or two forms. The spelling rules that govern these roots, furthermore, are largely consistent.

Did You Know?

The Latin base *pung, punct* means to "pierce" and gives us such words as *pungent* (smells and tastes that "pierce" our senses); *puncture* (to "pierce" a hole); *punctuation* (the periods, commas, and apostrophes that we form by "piercing" the paper with dot-like strokes); and *punctual* ("on the dot," i.e., the "pierce" mark). This same base has a French variant in *poign, point* (note the diphthong *oi* in place of the single Latin *u*). Thus, the word *poignant* is cognate with this family. *Poignant* feelings are emotionally "piercing," and we feel them keenly. Get the *point*?

THE FRENCH CONNECTION IN SPELLING

Because many Latin words have entered English through French, several bases have undergone slight spelling modifications. Such changes are often recognizable because French has a preference for diphthongs (two vowel sounds in the same syllable, such as *ou* in *pound*), whereas Latin prefers a single vowel followed by a consonant, as in *posit* and *composite*. This is why Latin *pon, pos, posit* and the French version, *pound*, are all cognates. When a Latin base exhibits a fourth form, often containing a diphthong, that form is usually from French.

It is beneficial for students to learn these four slightly variant forms as all expressing the basic idea of "put, place": *opponents* "put, place" themselves "against" a challenger; we *pose* for a picture by "placing" ourselves in a flattering *position*; we produce *compounds* when we "put" words "together"; we "put" "down" money when we make a *deposit*; stray dogs are caught and "put" in *pounds*. The words go on and on, but the few forms of the base remain constant.

The Latin base *pung, punct* means to "pierce" and gives us such words as *pungent* (smells and tastes that "pierce" our senses); *puncture* (to "pierce" a hole); *punctuation* (the periods, commas, and apostrophes that we form by "piercing" the paper with dot-like strokes); and *punctual* ("on the dot," i.e., the "pierce" mark). This same base has a French variant in *poign, point* (note the diphthong *oi* in place of the single Latin *u*). Thus, the word *poignant* is cognate with this family. *Poignant* feelings are emotionally "piercing," and we feel them keenly. Get the *point*?

SUMMARY

Every English word provides three kinds of information that can support spelling: alphabetic, pattern, and meaning. Moreover, recognizing letter patterns helps students connect both sound and meaning as they encounter new vocabulary. If teachers are aware of this, they can easily draw attention to many spelling patterns as they present specific prefixes, suffixes, and bases. In this chapter, we have shared some of the spelling tips included in many lessons of the *Building Vocabulary* curriculum to help students understand how the meaning of a word and its spelling are connected. Understanding that there is a spelling-meaning (as well as a spelling-sound) connection is an important linguistic concept whether you teach spelling as a separate subject or one root at a time.

CHAPTER 10

The Story of English—How Did We Get Here?

Knowing one's history is important, whether it is personal, family, community, or cultural history. Knowledge of where we have been can help us better understand who and where we are today and perhaps provide insights into what the future may hold. Languages have interesting histories as well. English, in particular, has a fascinating history. In fact, it has multiple histories because it has multiple sources. These various sources have informed and profoundly influenced the English we speak, read, and write today.

Before setting out on our brief tour of English, here are some interesting facts about the language. Of the thousands of languages spoken around the world, English is arguably the most pervasive. It is the international language of business, government, technology, science, and the arts. It is used on every continent and is an important language in well over 80 countries (Brook 1998). More than a billion people speak it. Even in countries with no significant historical ties to England or the United States, the study of English is often a requirement for high school graduation. Many universities throughout the world insist on a perfunctory knowledge of English for admission into undergraduate and graduate programs. They also require advanced study of English at the college level, since it is assumed that educated professionals will be coming into contact with written and spoken English throughout their studies and careers. On an international level, business and diplomatic transactions between people of different countries are often conducted in English as the "lingua franca," or common language. Worldwide, the English language is associated with education, progress, commerce, diplomacy, and advancement on many levels.

Not only is English a widely used language around the globe, it is also a deep language. By deep, we mean that it has more words than any other modern language (Brook 1998). Though English has more than a billion words, only about a fifth of them are used regularly. Still, that is more than double the number of words used on a regular basis in many of the Romance languages, to cite just one linguistic family. The rich depth of the English vocabulary is directly attributable to its breadth: English speakers who have come into contact with other cultures throughout modern history—through travel, trade, cultural exchanges, and military conquests—have absorbed artifacts, products, concepts, and modes of expression into their own language. It would be fair to suggest that the English vocabulary is a melting pot of words from around the world. Did you know, for example, the word *ketchup* is derived from Chinese, the word *chocolate* comes from Aztec, the word *algebra* comes from Arabic, and the word *khaki* comes from Persian? Speakers of English have proven to be excellent listeners and adapters, freely taking new words into this ever-growing language family. But the most significant contributors to the English vocabulary have been the ancient Greeks and Romans. In this chapter, we explain how two erroneously named "dead languages" came to provide more than 70 percent of the words in the English dictionary and more than 90 percent of English words of two or more syllables (Brunner 2004).

These few facts provide those of us who teach English with some important insights. First, we see that a solid grounding in English, in its spoken and written forms, is important both for our students and for us who, as teachers, aim to model lifelong learning for our students. For students to be successful in school and in their adult lives beyond the years of their formal education, they must learn English—and they must learn it well. Second, the broad scope and deep history of the English vocabulary mean that an English-speaking student has a daunting number of words to master. Teachers are charged with the instruction of literally thousands of words that are essential to an understanding of all the content areas in a curriculum: social studies, politics, government, the natural sciences, mathematics, literature, the humanities, technology, the fine arts, and even the vocational arts. Without the words, students cannot learn the material. The very richness of English thus poses vast possibilities but also poses special challenges to students and teachers alike.

As we broaden and deepen our own and our students' vocabularies, we become increasingly "word conscious," or interested in vocabulary for vocabulary's sake. The ancient Greek statesman and philosopher Solon of Athens (594 BC) wrote, "I grow old ever learning." This adage applies to everyone, but most of all to teachers. Our language is ever evolving, adding new words every day. We, too, are perpetually learning. But how did our language come about?

The Romano-Celtic Period: 58 BC–AD 450

Despite its current importance, English comes from humble origins. The history of English is largely a history of England itself and the peoples who came to that island from the western coast of Europe (McCrum, Cran, and MacNeil 1987). The original settlers of England were the Celts, ancestors of people who now live in Scotland, Ireland, Wales, and Brittany in France. The Celts, who spoke a language known as Gaelic, had been living in England for several hundred years when Julius Caesar and his Roman legions invaded Gaul (modern-day Switzerland and France) in 58 BC. By the first century AD, the Romans had crossed the English Channel and occupied Britain as well. Unable to conquer the entire British Isle and attempting to fend off the hostile Celts to the north, the emperor Hadrian erected Hadrian's Wall in AD 122, thereby putting an end to Rome's northward territorial expansion. The Romans remained in England until 410, when they withdrew their last appointed governing official.

This 400-year period was crucial to the linguistic development of the people whose descendants would eventually become speakers of modern English. When the Romans occupied Gaul and Britain, they brought with them their own language, Latin (Ayers 1986). Especially in cities and towns, Latin was imposed as the language of public administration and also became the language of everyday communication. As the Roman soldiers commingled with the indigenous populations, the so-called Romance languages (i.e., Roman based) were born: French, Italian, Portuguese, Romanian, and Spanish. The military nature of this commingling is still evident in such place names as Greenwich ("Green Village": the suffix –wich is from Latin vicus, meaning "village" [think of the word vicar]) and Winchester ("Win Camp": the suffix –chester is from Latin castra, meaning "camp"). In outlying areas and in the countryside, by contrast, the native people spoke their own various Celtic dialects, resulting in a peaceful coexistence of two language groups. The very

name of London (ancient Lugdunum) is derived from the Celtic word *dunum*, meaning "hill fortress" (think of high sand *dunes*).

During this bilingual Romano-Celtic period, a pattern emerged: the Celtic dialects provided the names of common and familiar everyday objects and places, while Latin provided the names for the many inventions and technological advancements that the Romans brought with them. For the most part, the Celtic words were monosyllabic, while Latin—a highly inflected language—provided the longer words. Outstanding engineers, the Romans built paved roads wherever they went (which is why we say "all roads lead to Rome"). They constructed elaborate aqueducts to bring potable water from the mountains into public living areas. As they expanded the economy, they built large *villas* (a Latin word) to oversee the farmers who worked the estates. The crops they produced would be not only consumed by the locals but also exported to other parts of the empire. All these new things introduced by the Romans also brought in new words. Thus, along with the Roman roads themselves, the Latin word for paved street, *via strata*, came into the Romance languages (e.g., Italian *strada*) and also into English (*street*). The indigenous populations had never seen aqueducts or villas before. Their vocabularies expanded as the Romans modernized their lives.

But the Romans brought more than roads, aqueducts, villas, and armies into Britain. They also brought the cultural inheritance of the Greeks. When Rome defeated ancient Greece and reduced it to the status of a province in 144 BC, the Latin poet Horace wrote, "We have conquered Greece, but Greece has imposed her arts on rustic Latium" (Horace, c. 14 BC). The earliest example of Roman literature (273 BC) was a Latin translation of Homer's *Odyssey*, intended for use as a text for Roman schoolchildren. The same translator, a slave named Livius Andronicus, also translated Greek plays into Latin so that the Romans could enjoy them. In the visual arts, Roman sculptors learned their skills by making copies of Greek statues. The study of ancient Roman culture is, in many ways, the study of the translation of Greek culture into Latin. Nearly all the various disciplines that lie at the core of any educational system today can be traced back to Greece: the words *school*, *poetry*, *drama*, *tragedy*, *comedy*, *theater*, *philosophy*, *theology*, *history*, *technology*, *biology*, *chemistry*, *physics*, *geometry*, *anatomy*, *astronomy*, *mathematics*, *biography*, *politics*, and *democracy* are all derived from Greek.

Thus, when the Romans occupied the Western world, they brought in a Greco-Roman culture that had words for things that the indigenous populations had never even imagined. This is why the so-called higher pursuits of education are directly connected to an understanding of the Greek and Latin foundation of English vocabulary. The word *translate* is from Latin, meaning "to carry across." The Romans were *translators* in every sense of the word. They carried Greek culture into Latin, and they carried this culture into Europe and England (Green 2008). This is why more than 70 percent of the words in an English dictionary are from Greek and Latin bases and why more than 90 percent of all English words of two or more syllables are of the same classical origins.

Old English: AD 450-1066

In the middle of the fourth century, West Germanic tribes who spoke a Low German dialect akin to modern Saxon moved into the areas occupied by the Romans and the Celts. In 450, after a series of pirate raids along the British coast, these tribes of Angles (who eventually gave their name to England), Saxons (hence the term *Anglo-Saxon*), and Jutes occupied Britain and established the first Germanic settlement there. They called this area the Kingdom of Kent. The original Celts were driven to the fringes of Scotland and Wales, to nearby Ireland, and to Brittany on continental Europe. It is in the commingling of the Anglo-Saxon invaders of Britain with the now-Romanized culture they found there—with its Greek- and Latin-based vocabulary—that the English language was born. We call this initial stage Old English. It may interest you to know that in many American universities during the first half of the 20th century, students who aspired to become English teachers were required to take courses in German and Latin; the structure of English (its syntax, grammar, and pronunciation) is Germanic, but its vocabulary is Greco-Roman.

As we observed in our discussion of the Romano-Celtic period, a pattern similarly evolved during the Old English period. Most of the common words used in the daily lives of the Angles, Saxons, and Jutes come from Germanic roots of English. Words—again, primarily monosyllabic—such as *fire, fight, high, knob, foot, knuckle, knee, wrist, hate, wrong, help, love, meat, we, wife, sheep, ox, earth, hill, land, dog, wood, field, work, sun, moon, here*, and *there* come from the original Anglo-Saxon-Jute invasion of England. Latinate vocabulary, by contrast, was used for words of higher concern.

Saint Augustine brought Christianity to the island in 597. As with the original Romans under Julius Caesar, a building program ensued. Churches and monasteries were erected, and clergy were imported. Besides serving as places of worship, these buildings also housed students and educators. The first classical curricula were established in such disciplines as poetry, grammar, astronomy, mathematics, and rhetoric. (This is why many college and university campuses resemble cloistered monasteries and why the academic regalia of caps and gowns recall early Christian monks.) Much of this instruction was conducted in Latin and, to a lesser extent, in Greek and Hebrew. In the late fourth century, St. Jerome translated the original Greek and Hebrew Bible into Latin; this is known as the Vulgate Bible, meaning "the Bible for the masses," and it was used as a language textbook by educators as well as a source of religious instruction.

Church-related words, such as *altar, ark, candle, cross, crucify, inundation* (from Noah and the flood), *congregation, mass, minister, disciple, redemption, sacrifice, shrine, silk, priest, bishop, vestments, temple,* and *beatitude,* come from the Latin Vulgate (the Latin translation of the Bible). Also included in this list are many Greek-based words that were translated into Latin, such as *angel, apostle, epistle, psalter,* and *psalms.* Hebrew words such as *Sabbath* and words of Middle Eastern origin such as *camel, cedar,* and *myrrh* were also integrated into English.

Once again, we observe the profound effect of linguistic and cultural translation on the creation and growth of the English language. The advent of Christianity in England had an impact even on some of the original Germanic words brought by the Angles, Saxons, and Jutes. The words *God, heaven,* and *hell* are Germanic words that took on deeper meaning with Christianity. The Greek word *evangelium,* which means "good news," was transformed into the Germanic *god-spell,* from which our word *gospel* comes. Similarly, the Latin *Spiritus Sanctus,* which means "Holy Spirit," became the Germanic *Halig Gast,* which eventually evolved into *Holy Ghost.*

Although the invasion of the British Isles by the Angles, Saxons, and Jutes led to the birth of English, the English that has evolved would be scarcely recognizable to English speakers of today. One of the greatest impetuses to the evolution of English came from the other peoples and their languages that touched English. When other people invaded England, they brought their own languages that melded with the English that was spoken at the time to create a new form of English.

The Angles, Saxons, and Jutes were not the last to conquer and settle in England. More invasions were to follow. Next to invade were the Scandinavians, also known as Vikings, Norsemen, or Danes, who began to arrive in 787. The Danes occupied the northern part of England, leaving the southern part to remain predominantly Germanic or Anglo-Saxon. Until 1050, the Danes intermarried and mixed with the Anglo-Saxons, leading to a mixing of the two languages. Unlike the Celts, who were vanquished and whose language had little impact on the language brought over by the Anglo-Saxons, the Anglo-Saxons created a form of English that did not disappear. This version of English was greatly influenced by the Scandinavian language of the Danes. English words such as *hit, leg, low, root, scalp, scatter, scare, scold, scrape, skin, skirt, skit, sky, same,* and *want* are all of Scandinavian descent. Again, we observe that these words are largely monosyllabic and refer to daily things and events.

The marriage and evolution of the Germanic and the Scandinavian languages in England, from approximately 500 to 1200, gave rise to Old English. However, a new conquest of England was about to occur that would change the language once again. This one did not come from the north, but from the south.

Middle English: 1066–1500

In 1066, the Normans from France defeated King Harold and the Anglo-Saxon English at the Battle of Hastings, initiating a new phase in the development of English. King Harold was the last English-speaking ruler of England for nearly three hundred years. The Norman French, led by King William, took complete control of the English government. For the next several generations, official activities were conducted in French. But let us recall that French itself is a Romance language, the product of Julius Caesar's original conquest of Gaul (the land that includes present-day France) and the subsequent commingling of Roman soldiers with the local inhabitants. Many English words that refer to the government and the law are of French origin, and they entered the English language during the Norman conquest of England. Words such as *authority, attorney, council, empire, felony, judge, jury, liberty, mayor, nobility, parliament, prince, treaty,* and *treasurer* are derived from French words that themselves are of Latin origin. Thus, during the period in which Middle English evolved, we see a doubling of the impact of Latin: the Latin of Julius Caesar's troops, followed by the Latinized French of the Norman invaders and rulers.

Did You Know?

The most important text in Old English is the epic tale of *Beowulf*. Here are its first three lines, taken from an original text at Fordham University. Can you read them?

HWÆT, WE GAR-DEna in geardagum,
þeodcyninga þrym gefrunon,
hu ða æþelingas ellen fremedon!

Neither can we, but here is a translation by Francis Gummere:

LO, praise of the prowess of people-kings
of spear-armed Danes, in days long sped,
we have heard, and what honor the athelings won!

By this time, the Latin language had been well established as the principal language in which the affairs of religion and the Christian church were conducted. Since most formal education was conducted through the church, Latin remained the language of education and academia. The enrichment of the English vocabulary by Greco-Latin words was continuing, and the role of Greco-Latin vocabulary as the language of education was established. The common people of England, the original Anglo-Saxons, continued to speak in their original language while learning, unavoidably, some French. The French rulers relied on their native language, while learning only enough English to give orders to their English subjects. The English speakers, by contrast, were absorbing all these words, which were, for the most part, of Latin origin. Imagine how rich the linguistic environment of England was during this period! Three languages were in use at one time, spoken and written for three distinct purposes—French for government, Latin (and translated Greek) for religion and education, and indigenous English for everyday conversation.

As for English itself, its structure and syntax remained largely unchanged as an Anglo-Saxon tongue. But with its longstanding tradition of openness to other cultures, its vocabulary grew exponentially as it absorbed the cultural influences of the Latin-speaking church and the French overlords. This is one of the most remarkable features of our language. We have different words from different sources to express a wide range of concepts on various levels of discourse. Although this intermingling of languages has resulted in a complicated language in terms of pronunciation and spelling (for example, the silent *k* in the words *knight* and *knee* and the British spelling of *colour*), it has also resulted in an English that is rich in its ability to communicate shades of meaning.

One concept can often be expressed in different ways in English, each reflecting a different language source. For example, the Anglo-Saxon *fear* can be expressed as *terror* in French (originally Latin) and *trepidation* in Latin. In many cases, these semantically related words carry a difference in sense. For example, the monosyllabic *win* in Anglo-Saxon is an all-purpose word (e.g., we can *win* the lottery, *win* a race, or cultivate charming and *winning* ways). The French-based equivalent, *succeed*, means literally "to come up from under" (e.g., one king *succeeds* another; an American *success* story about reaching fame after overcoming poverty). The Latin *triumph* carries a connotation of swaggering after a major victory or overcoming an extremely formidable foe. The Anglo-Saxon word *kingly* can also be communicated as *royal* and *sovereign* in French and as *regal* in Latin. We thus have the option of any number of expressions: we can speak of a *kingly* demeanor, a *royal* feast fit for a king, a *sovereign* ruler, and the *regal* furnishings of a palace or someone's sumptuous living room. Clearly, although French and Latin have made the original Anglo-Saxon English much more complex, the ability to communicate with deeper and more subtle nuances has been enhanced through the adoption of these culturally rich vocabularies.

Although the French Normans ruled lands in France and England after the Battle of Hastings, by the early 13th century, landholders in both countries were forced to declare their allegiance to either France or England. In 1244, the King of France pronounced that "as it is impossible that any man living in my kingdom, and having possessions in England, can competently serve two masters, he must either inseparably attach himself to me or to the King of England." This separation meant that although French-speaking men of French origin still ruled England, their ultimate allegiance was to England, not France. Thus, the French language, although well established in England, did not supplant the Anglo-Saxon English spoken by the everyday people.

The sense of nationalism that arose as the nobility in England declared themselves Englishmen or Frenchmen, combined with the Hundred Years War (1337–1454), allowed Anglo-Saxon English to remain the dominant language of the island. But the English that evolved during this period—now called Middle English—incorporated the rich French and Latin vocabulary of the occupier. In 1356, when the mayor of London declared that all court proceedings were to be held in English instead of French, the English language itself was replete with borrowed words that dealt with law, government, and other official dealings. Furthermore, in 1362, the transactions of the British Parliament were conducted in English, not French. During the rise of Middle English, therefore, Latin-based vocabulary embedded itself even more deeply.

Geoffrey Chaucer (1343–1400), who wrote *The Canterbury Tales*, lived during this time. Here are the first several lines from "The Knight's Tale," written in Middle English, taken from Harvard University. See whether you can figure them out. (The translation is provided in the chapter summary.)

> **Whilom, as olde stories tellen us,**
> **Ther was a duc that highte Theseus;**
> **Of Atthenes he was lord and governour,**
> **And in his tyme swich a conquerour**
> **That gretter was ther noon under the sonne.**

How did you do? Was this easier to read than the Old English excerpt from *Beowulf* on page 143? What do you notice about Middle English word order? Do you see what might be a French influence on spelling?

The stage was now set for the Renaissance.

Modern English: 1500–Present

The beginning of modern English can be traced to the Renaissance. The term *Renaissance*—a French word of Latin origin—means "rebirth" and refers to the rediscovery of the ancient western civilizations of Greece and Rome. Beginning in Italy, the reawakening of intellectual interest in the cultural achievements of the classical Greeks in particular quickly spread throughout Europe and into England. The Renaissance was an exciting period of invention, discovery, creativity, and exploration for the entire Western world. The Renaissance reintroduced Europe to the scientific knowledge and writings of the Greeks and Romans. Thus, English was given a third exposure to Latin. This time, however, the European scholars were not content to rely on Latin translations of the works they were studying. They insisted on returning to the Greek language itself. This is how so many Greek-based words related to science and technology were introduced into English. Students of medicine and anatomy returned to the original writings of Hippocrates, the ancient Greek father of medicine. Students of geometry began reading Euclid in the original Greek. Philosophers and theologians turned to Plato and Aristotle, while poets and dramatists read Homer, Sophocles, and Euripides in ancient Greek. Such academic, scientific, technical, and medical words as *atmosphere*, *atom*, *catalyst*, *analysis*, *trigonometry*, *trapezoid*, *capsule*, *catastrophe*, *lexicon*, *pneumonia*, *skeleton*, and *thermometer* come directly from Greek. By the 18th century, European and British scholars were so taken with the study of Greece that a new intellectual movement began, *philhellenism*, which means "the love of things Greek." British poet Percy Bysshe Shelley (1792–1822) wrote in his preface to "Hellas," "We are all Greeks. Our laws, our literature, our religion, our arts have their roots in Greece." This is an amazing statements from an Englishman who found his intellectual identity in the study of Greece. The English people and the English language have an age-old tradition of respecting, adopting, and transmitting the legacies of Greece and Rome.

Words from other lands and languages that were immersed in the Renaissance also influenced English. From French came more words such as *bigot* and *detail*, from Italian came *portico* and *stucco*, from Spanish words such as *desperado* and *embargo*, and from the Low Countries (coastal northwest Europe), *smuggle* and *reef*. The Renaissance was indeed a time of new words for English. During this period, between 10,000 and 12,000 words were added to the language.

In 1476, the printing press was introduced into England by William Caxton. Books became less expensive and more abundant. Between 1500 and 1640, 20,000 books, pamphlets, and broadsheets were published, a 50 percent increase over what had been published in all of Europe before 1500. Thus, an ever-increasing number of English people were learning to read and write. English was expanding, not only in terms of number of words, but also as a written and oral language that was used by a growing number of people.

In 1604, King James commissioned a new translation of the Bible into English. The English vocabulary that appears in this text owes its very existence to the Vulgate Latin Bible that St. Jerome had produced some 1,200 years earlier. By now, the effect of Greek and Latin vocabulary had made an indelible impression on the English language. From the King James Version (*version* means "translation") come several expressions that are current even today: *the apple of his eye*, *salt of the earth*, *fruit of the womb*, *out of the mouths of babes*, and *baptism by fire*. This level of English was not restricted to those who could read and write. The sacred texts were read aloud during church services, and the English-speaking public absorbed all this rich vocabulary simply by listening.

In addition to the King James Version of the Bible, another cultural marvel appeared as Modern English was born: William Shakespeare (1564–1616). With his tragedies, comedies, poems, and sonnets, Shakespeare entertained both the nobility and the masses with his enormous talent for *neologizing*. He actually created new words in English. He used nearly 18,000 different words in his entire body of work—a remarkable range of vocabulary for his time. Of these words, close to 10 percent were of his own invention. Shakespeare's education included training in the classics and rhetoric, both of which are rooted in the Greek and Latin languages. In particular, he was fascinated with classical myths as recorded in the Roman poet Ovid's long poem, *Metamorphoses*, to which he turned for inspiration for many of his plots. Shakespeare was also an avid reader of Latin poetry. Thus, we find yet another instance of the impact of Latin on English. When Shakespeare coined new words, he combined the already-existing Greek and Latin roots that he knew by heart. Words such as *baseless, bedroom, dishearten, dislocate, impartial, indistinguishable, invulnerable, lonely, metamorphosis, monumental, premeditated, reliance, sanctimonious*, and *submerge* are examples of the many words Shakespeare created to express meaning and engage his language-sensitive listeners.

The New World: English on the Move

The history of English is not only the story of the various peoples who invaded England and brought their languages with them. It is also the story of English-speaking people traveling and emigrating abroad and acquiring words from the speakers of the lands they visited. The Renaissance was not only a time of rebirth for the ancient Greek and Roman classics; it was also the time period during which England emerged as a world-class maritime power, surpassing the Spanish. The English people and their language began moving out and making their way into other lands around the globe.

Did You Know?

Although you have probably seen and studied these lines from Shakespeare's *Hamlet* many times in the past, this time we ask you to look at the language. We guess that this will be much easier for you to read than *The Canterbury Tales*. Why? How do the words and word order compare to Middle English? What evidence do you find of figurative language?

To be or not to be, that is the question;
Whether 'tis nobler in the mind to suffer
The slings and arrows of outrageous fortune,
Or to take arms against a sea of troubles,
And by opposing, end them.

(Shakespeare, *Hamlet*, Act III, scene ii)

A large part of this cultural, political, and commercial expansion focused on the original American colonies of the New World, beginning with the settlement of Jamestown, Virginia, by the London Company in 1607. In 1620, the Puritans created another colony in Massachusetts. These colonists brought with them their English culture, traditions, religion, and their language. English became the dominant language of the colonies and subsequently of the new nation that was to be formed from the colonies. As the Puritans sought to educate their children, they used the King James Bible, with its rich Latinate vocabulary. In this way, the Greek and Latin roots of English vocabulary spread to North America and took permanent hold.

Beyond the original colonies, the English people and their language have circled the globe. "The sun never sets on the British Empire" was the motto at the time. English is spoken and read around the globe by millions of people. It has influenced the development and history of nations around the world. It has also had an impact on many other languages. However, in the same way that English has influenced other people, lands, and languages, it has also been influenced itself by the people, lands, and languages it has touched. There is hardly a country or a culture in the world today that has not had an impact on the English language.

English was influenced by the American Indians living in the Americas during the time of English colonization. Words such as *hickory*, *moose*, *skunk*, and *tobacco* are English words that owe their origins to the American Indians who inhabited North America during this period of colonization. Many place names on the North American continent, such as Massachusetts, Ohio, Illinois, Chicago, Omaha, Mississippi, and Dakota, come from the original North Americans. From the Caribbean, discovered by New World explorers, words such as *hammock* and *hurricane* have entered English. From Africa, English has absorbed *yam*, *banana*, and *canary*. Australia, too, was at one time a colony of England. This is why English is the official language of Australia. As in North America, English was influenced by the language spoken by the native peoples living on the Australian continent at the time of colonization. Words such as *boomerang* and *kangaroo* come from the native Australians and later became adopted as English words. (See Appendix D for many more examples of words absorbed into English.)

Learning English Today: The Lessons of History

The English language has a complex and fascinating history. Little wonder, then, that the study of English words is an enriching experience for all our students. The modern English spoken and written today is the result of the influences and blending of many other languages that touched and even dominated England. To this day, new words are being added or assimilated into English from other languages and cultures that English-speaking people have encountered. The assimilative nature of English has resulted in a rich and complex language—one that is filled with new words ready to express both complex and subtle ideas. However, this richness and complexity can also make English a challenging language to pronounce, spell, and define.

Although English bears the impact of every language it has encountered, it is especially indebted to Greek and Latin for the richness of its vocabulary. As this brief survey has made clear, the indebtedness of English to Latin dates back to the first century BC, when Julius Caesar crossed the Alps, entered ancient Gaul, and crossed over into Britain. With their troops, the Romans brought Latin into Europe and England, and they also brought the translated culture of the ancient Greeks, whom they admired and respected for their achievements in the letters, sciences, and arts. This culture became even more pronounced during the Renaissance, when Europeans rediscovered the ancient Greeks and enriched their vocabularies with words taken directly from Greek, without relying on Latin translators. All this time, church education was rooted in the spiritual and academic vocabulary of the Greek Bible and its subsequent translation into Latin. This tradition continued with the King James Bible, which brought a veritable flood of Latin words into English. To this day, students intent on mastering the many content areas of a school curriculum find themselves returning to the ancients and their languages. Far from "dead," Greek and Latin continue to infuse and revitalize an ever-evolving language.

SUMMARY

At the outset of this chapter, we commented on the daunting task teachers face in covering such an enormous word system as the English language! But as we review the history of this language and understand how systematic it has been in incorporating Greek- and Latin-based words, we may see a glimmer of light. With a systematic approach to these Greek and Latin word elements, we can begin to sort through the confusing array of word lists and face our teaching mission with excitement and confidence. This book is dedicated to helping teachers and students make the most of the Greek and Latin origins of English words as they teach and learn our language.

As promised on page 145, here is the translation of "The Knight's Tale":

> Once, as old histories tell us,
> There was a duke who was called Theseus;
> He was lord and governor of Athens,
> And in his time such a conqueror
> That there was no one greater under the sun.

Resources for Students

This section provides brief descriptions of several types of resources for students: general websites, children's books that focus on word play, and children's dictionaries.

Websites for Students

Learning Vocabulary Fun! — www.vocabulary.co.il

There is something here for all ages and skill levels. Students can play Match Game and Hangman or do crossword puzzles, word searches, and jumbles. All the activities are for one player.

Surfing the Net with Kids — www.surfnetkids.com/games

This site contains free kids' games listed by type (e.g., crossword, jigsaw), topic (e.g., science, geography), or theme (e.g., sports, dress-up, holidays). It also has an easy-to-use search tool.

Vocabulary University — www.vocabulary.com

This site is full of puzzles and other activities based on Greek and Latin roots. The puzzles change regularly, so students can visit the site frequently without getting bored.

Word Central — www.wordcentral.com

Maintained by *Merriam-Webster*, this site has plenty of activities and information for students as well as resources (including lesson plans) for teachers. You can even build your own dictionary.

K–5 Books for Word Play

Cleary, Brian P. 1999. *A Mink, a Fink, a Skating Rink: What Is a Noun?* Minneapolis, MN: Carolrhoda.

Cleary, Brian P. 2001. *To Root, To Toot, To Parachute: What Is a Verb?* Minneapolis, MN: Carolrhoda.

Cleary, Brian P. 2004. *Pitch and Throw, Grasp and Know: What Is a Synonym?* Minneapolis, MN: Carolrhoda.

Cleary, Brian P. 2006. *Stop and Go, Yes and No: What Is an Antonym?* Minneapolis, MN: Carolrhoda.

Frasier, Debra. 2000. *Miss Alaineus: A Vocabulary Disaster*. San Diego, CA: Harcourt.

Gwynne, Fred. 1976. *A Chocolate Moose for Dinner*. New York: Aladdin.

Gwynne, Fred. 1987. *The King Who Rained*. New York: Aladdin.

Leedy, Loreen, and Pat Street. *There's a Frog in My Throat! 440 Animal Sayings a Little Bird Told Me*. New York: Holiday House.

Parish, Herman, and Peggy Parish. Amelia Bedelia series. New York: HarperCollins.

Terban, Marvin. 1982. *Scholastic Dictionary of Idioms*. New York: Scholastic.

Terban, Marvin. 1996. *Eight Ate: A Feast of Homonym Riddles*. New York: Clarion.

Walden, Brandon. 2018. *Seeds and Trees*. Redding, CA: Treasured Tree.

Student Dictionaries

Little Explorers English Picture Dictionary — www.enchantedlearning.com /Dictionary.html

Click on a letter of the alphabet, and your students will find dozens of words that begin with that letter. Each word has a picture and a definition. Best of all, this site also has picture dictionaries that go from English to Spanish, French, Italian, Portuguese, German, Swedish, Dutch, and Japanese. These dictionaries will captivate all your students and provide extra support to English learners. (**Note:** Older students may enjoy working with some of the other electronic dictionaries and resources listed in the Teacher Resources section of this chapter.)

DK Children's Illustrated Dictionary. 1994. New York: DK Children. For ages 4–8.

Merriam-Webster Children's Dictionary. 2005. New York: DK Publishing. For ages 4–8.

My First Dictionary. 1993. New York: DK Children. For ages 4–8.

Scholastic Children's Dictionary. 2002. New York: Scholastic. For ages 4–8.

Resources for Teachers

This section contains resources to enhance vocabulary instruction: websites for lists of words and roots, websites to create vocabulary games and puzzles, electronic dictionaries and other resources, and sites that offer lesson plans related to vocabulary.

Websites for Word Roots/Word Lists

Building Vocabulary — www.learner.org/jnorth/tm/tips/Tip0023.html

Sponsored by Journey North, this site has quick and easy classroom vocabulary activities.

Most Frequently Used Words Lists — www.esldesk.com/esl-quizzes/frequently -used-english-words/words.htm

This useful site provides the 1,000 most frequently used words in the English language.

Word Study — www.timrasinski.com

In his website, Dr. Timothy Rasinski provides resources and a monthly blog in which he discusses issues related to foundational reading or provides seasonal word-study lessons that teachers can use immediately with students.

Word Roots and Prefixes — www.virtualsalt.com/roots.htm

This site has lists of roots and words that come from them.

Websites to Create Word Games

Discovery Education's Puzzlemaker — puzzlemaker.discoveryeducation.com/WordSearchSetupForm.asp

This word-search generator gives options for letter use and word type. The crisscross option is a crossword puzzle maker.

SuperKids Word Search Puzzles — www.superkids.com/aweb/tools/words/

Make your own printable hidden word puzzles using the SuperKids Word Search Puzzle Creator. Hangman and several other puzzle types are also available. (Only available for PCs.)

Word Search — www.armoredpenguin.com/wordsearch

You can use the "generator" to create your own word jumbles and puzzles.

Dictionaries and Reference Websites

AllWords.com — www.allwords.com

This site has an online dictionary that does a multilingual search, which is very useful for students who are learning English as a second language. "Links for Word Lovers" will take you to all kinds of resources for information (dictionaries, thesauri, etymologies) and word play (puns, rhymes, songs, quotations).

Lexico — www.lexico.com/en

A free online dictionary from the makers of the famous Oxford English Dictionary. The site includes word games and other support materials for spelling, grammar, etymology, and foreign phrases, plus an "Ask the Experts" link where you can find answers to frequently asked language questions. **Note:** A Spanish dictionary is also available at this site.

A Word a Day — www.wordsmith.org/awad

Have a new word come straight into your email every day! This site also provides a vocabulary word, its definition, pronunciation information with audio clip, etymology, usage example, and quotation. Subscription is free.

The Big List — www.wordorigins.org/index.php/big_list/

This site explains the origin of more than four hundred familiar words and phrases, selected because they are "interesting or because some bit of folklore, sometimes true and sometimes false, is associated with the origin." Dazzle students with your own knowledge, or let them explore for themselves.

Merriam-Webster Online — www.m-w.com

This site has an extensive and easy-to-use online dictionary and thesaurus that even provides audio pronunciations. Students will enjoy free word games and can sign up for Word of the Day.

One Look Dictionary Search — www.onelook.com

As described in Chapter 5, this site can be used to search and sort words. Type in a word, and let this site look it up in several dictionaries! It also has a "Reverse Dictionary." Type in a description of the concept, and it finds words and phrases that match it.

Online Etymology Dictionary — www.etymonline.com

Type in any word, and this dictionary will tell you its history.

Thesaurus.com — thesaurus.com

Type in a word, and quickly find synonyms and antonyms for it. This site also has a dictionary, an encyclopedia, and a word of the day in English and Spanish.

Education World — www.educationworld.com/a_lesson/lesson/lesson328.shtml

Many word wall activities are available on this site.

Read•Write•Think — www.readwritethink.org

This site, cosponsored by the International Literacy Association and the National Council of Teachers of English, contains lesson plans spanning all aspects of the language arts and all grade levels as well.

Further Professional Reading

Elaboration Techniques — www.ldonline.org/article/5759

This site describes a way to support vocabulary learning among students with learning disabilities.

American Heritage Dictionaries, eds. 2016. *100 Words Every High School Freshman Should Know*. Boston: Houghton Mifflin.

Beeler, Duane. 1988. *Book of Roots: A Full Study of Our Families of Words*. Chicago: Union Representative.

Funk, Charles. 2002. *Thereby Hangs a Tale: Stories of Curious Word Origins*. New York: Collins.

Funk, Wilfred. 1992. *Word Origins: An Exploration and History of Words and Language*. San Antonio, TX: Wings Books. (Originally published in 1950.)

Jack, Albert. 2005. *Red Herrings and White Elephants: The Origins of Phrases We Use Every Day*. New York: HarperCollins.

Liberman, Anatoly. 2005. *Word Origins and How We Know Them*. New York: Oxford University Press.

Teacher Resource Books, Lesson Plans, and Curriculum

Allen, Janet. 1999. *Words, Words, Words: Teaching Vocabulary in Grades 4–12*. Portland, ME: Stenhouse. A fourth-grade teacher shares dozens of wonderful and easy-to-implement strategies ready for duplicating.

Beck, Isabel L., Margaret G. McKeown, and Linda Kucan. 2002. *Bringing Words to Life: Robust Vocabulary Instruction*. 2nd ed. New York: Guilford. Explains a three-tier system for choosing and teaching vocabulary for reading comprehension.

Blachowicz, Camille, and Peter J. Fisher. 2015. *Teaching Vocabulary in All Classrooms*. 5th ed. Upper Saddle River, NJ: Merrill/Prentice-Hall. Each chapter is full of classroom-tested strategies. Topics include content-area vocabulary, integrating reading and writing, learning from context, using reference sources, word play, and assessment.

Brand, Max. 2004. *Word Savvy: Integrated Vocabulary, Spelling, and Word Study, Grades 3–6*. Portland, ME: Stenhouse. A fifth-grade teacher describes how he weaves word study throughout the day. He also provides advice and many specific examples that are easily adaptable to the primary grades.

Brassell, Danny, and James Flood. 2004. *Vocabulary Strategies Every Teacher Needs to Know*. San Diego, CA: Academic Professional Development. Contains 25 strategies, some familiar and some new, with easy-to-follow instructions and easy-to-duplicate templates.

Bromley, Karen. 2007. *Stretching Students' Vocabulary*. New York: Scholastic. The author offers a wealth of teacher-tested activities designed to help all learners master words for all subject areas.

Carris, Joan Davenport. 1994. *Peterson's Success with Words*. Princeton, NJ: Peterson's Guides. This workbook has hundreds of root words and "context" activities based on vocabulary needed for success on the SAT and similar standardized tests. The activities are fun to do, and the explanations are very clear. (These are better for older students.)

Fitzgerald, Jill, and Michael F. Graves. 2004. *Scaffolding Reading Experiences for English-Language Learners*. Norwood, MA: Christopher Gordon. The focus of this text is on teaching reading to second-language learners; it includes excellent suggestions for how to introduce these students to new vocabulary.

Fry, Edward Bernard. 2004. *The Vocabulary Teacher's Book of Lists*. San Francisco, CA: Jossey-Bass. Lists of words from content areas such as mathematics and science to word study with prefixes, roots, and homophones.

Garg, Anu, and Stuti Garg. 2003. *A Word a Day: A Romp through Some of the Most Unusual and Intriguing Words in English*. Hoboken, NJ: John Wiley & Sons. Sections include "Animal Words," "Latin Terms," "Words to Describe People," "Lesser-Known Counterparts of Everyday Words," and more.

Harmon, Janis, and Karen Wood. 2018. "The Vocabulary-Comprehension Relationship Across the Disciplines: Implications for Instruction." *Education Sciences* 8, no. 101. This paper discusses academic vocabulary, what is known about the vocabulary–comprehension relationship, a conceptualization of the intersection of academic vocabulary and the vocabulary–comprehension relationship, and the instructional implications emerging from this intersection.

Kamola, Lori. 2008. Successful Strategies for Reading in the Content Areas series. Huntington Beach, CA: Shell Education. Each book in this series has a detailed chapter about teaching vocabulary development strategies using nonfiction text. Many strategies are given, and graphic organizers are provided when appropriate.

Macceca, Stephanie. 2007. *Reading Strategies for Science*. Huntington Beach, CA: Shell Education. Learn practical standards-based strategies for teaching vocabulary in science. Each strategy includes specific instructions for differentiating instruction for English learners, gifted students, and struggling students.

Macceca, Stephanie. 2007. *Reading Strategies for Social Studies*. Huntington Beach, CA: Shell Education. Learn practical standards-based strategies for teaching vocabulary in social studies. Each strategy includes specific instructions for differentiating instruction for English learners, gifted students, and struggling students.

Macceca, Stephanie, and Trisha Brummer. 2008. *Reading Strategies for Mathematics*. Huntington Beach, CA: Shell Education. Learn practical standards-based strategies for teaching vocabulary in mathematics. Each strategy includes specific instructions for differentiating instruction for English learners, gifted students, and struggling students.

Padak, Nancy, Evangeline Newton, Timothy Rasinski, and Rick M. Newton. 2008. "Getting to the Root of Word Study: Teaching Latin and Greek Word Roots in Elementary and Middle Grades." In *What Research Has to Say about Vocabulary Instruction*, edited by Alan E. Farstrup and S. Jay Samuels, 6–31. Newark, DE: International Reading Association. This article gives background and guidelines on incorporating word-root study into the classroom.

Paynter, Diane E., Elena Bodrova, and Jane K. Doty. 2005. *For the Love of Words: Vocabulary Instruction That Works*. San Francisco, CA: Jossey-Bass. Practical ideas for expanding the role of vocabulary in reading, writing, and thinking.

Rasinski, Timothy. 2005. *Daily Word Ladders (Grades K–1, 1–2, 2–4)* and *Content Areas*. New York: Scholastic. Students will enjoy the challenge of "climbing" these developmentally appropriate (and easily duplicated) word ladders.

Rasinski, Timothy, and Roger Heym. *Making and Writing Words (Grades 2–3)*. Huntington Beach, CA: Shell Education. Over 40 ready-to-use word activities that help students improve their phonemic awareness, phonics, spelling, and vocabulary skills.

Rasinski, Timothy, Nancy Padak, and Gay Fawcett. 2010. *Effective Reading Strategies: Teaching Children Who Find Reading Difficult*. 4th ed. Boston, MA: Allyn and Bacon. Identifies strategies that target specific needs, including vocabulary and word study, of students who can use extra support in learning to read.

Rasinski, Timothy, Nancy Padak, Rick M. Newton, and Evangeline Newton. 2019. *Building Vocabulary: Foundations (Levels K–2)*. Huntington Beach, CA: Teacher Created Materials. Introduces students to a word family or root each week, with daily guided-practice activities. (Set includes Teacher's Guide, Student Guided Practice Book, Digital Resources, and Digital Games.)

Rasinski, Timothy, Nancy Padak, Rick M. Newton, and Evangeline Newton. 2020. *Building Vocabulary from Word Roots (Levels 3–8)*. Huntington Beach, CA: Teacher Created Materials. Introduces a new root each week, with daily guided-practice activities. (Set includes Teacher's Guide, Student Guided Practice Book, Digital Resources, and Digital Games.)

Rasinski, Timothy, Nancy Padak, Rick M. Newton, and Evangeline Newton. 2010. *Building Vocabulary from Word Roots (Levels 9–11)*. Huntington Beach, CA: Teacher Created Materials. Introduces a new root each week, with daily guided-practice activities.

Rasinski, Timothy, and William Rupley, eds. 2019. *Vocabulary Development*. Basel, Switzerland: MDPI. A collection of articles by various vocabulary scholars on the importance of vocabulary and effective instruction in vocabulary.

Stahl, Steven A. 1999. *Vocabulary Development*. Cambridge, MA: Brookline. An excellent review of what we know about vocabulary learning and what sort of instruction supports vocabulary development.

Commonly Taught Roots

The following roots chart will assist in vocabulary instruction. The first column provides a list of commonly taught Greek and Latin roots (including bases, prefixes, and suffixes); the second column provides the meaning of each root; and the third column provides sample words that utilize each root. The column of sample words is intended to give a sense of how the roots are used—it is by no means an exhaustive selection. These sample words are best used as a starting point for further developing vocabulary instruction. As students gain more proficiency with roots and root meanings, they will begin to come up with words on their own.

BASE	MEANING	EXAMPLE
adelph	brother	Philadelphia
aer(o)	air, wind	aerate, aerobic
ag, act, igu	drive, go	agile, action, ambiguous
agog(ue), agogy	lead	pedagogy, synagogue
al, alma	nourishing	alimony, alma mater
alg	pain, ache	analgesic, nostalgic
(a)llel	one another	parallel
am(i), amat, amor	love, friend	amiable, amateur, amorous
ambul	walk	ambulatory
angel	messenger	angelic
angle	angle, corner	quadrangle
anim	life, soul	animated
annu, enni	year	annual, perennial
anthrop	human being, humankind	anthropology
ap(i)	bee	apiary
aqu, aqua	water	aqueduct, aquatic
aquil	eagle	aquiline
astr(o)	star	astrology
athl	contest, struggle	athletics

BASE	MEANING	EXAMPLE
audi, audit	hear, listen	audience, audition
avi	bird	aviary, aviator
ball, bol	throw	ballistics, symbol
barbar	savage(ry)	barbarous
bell, bellum	war	bellicose, antebellum
bi	two	bicycle, biped
bibli(o)	book	bibliophile
bio	live, life	biology
bon, bene	good, well	bonanza, benevolent
bov	cow	bovine
brev	short	abbreviate
bys(s)	bottom	abyss, abysmal
can	dog	canine
cap, capt, cept, ceive	take, seize, get	captivity, receive, perception
caps	case	capsule
cardi	heart	cardiac
ced, ceed, cess	go, move, yield	recede, proceed, excess
celer	swift	accelerate
cent	one hundred	century
center, centr	center	eccentric
chrom	color	chromatic
chron(o)	time	chronic, chronology
cid, cis	cut, kill	genocide, excise
civ, cit, civil	city, citizen	civics, civilian, citadel
clam, clamat, claim	shout	proclamation, exclamatory, acclaim
class	classic	neoclassic
clin	lie, lean	recline

BASE	MEANING	EXAMPLE
clud, clus, clos	close, shut	exclude, inclusion, enclose
col	strain, sieve	colander, percolate
corn(u)	horn	cornucopia, unicorn
cosm(o)	world, order	cosmonaut, cosmetic
cotta	cooked, baked	terra-cotta
cred, credit	believe	incredible, accredited
cumb, cub	lie, lean	incubate, incumbent
cur, curs, cour, cours	run, go	concur, cursive, courier, concourse
cuss	hit, strike	concussion, percussion
cycl(e)	wheel	unicycle
dec, decim, decem	ten	decimal, December
dei, divin	god	deify, divinity
dem	the people	epidemic, democracy
dent	tooth, teeth	dentures
derm, dermat	skin	hypodermic, dermatitis
dexter, dextr	right hand	dexterity, ambidextrous
dic, dict	say, speak, tell	dictate, predict
dos(e), dot(e)	give	dosage, antidote
duc, duct	lead	induce, deduct
dynam, dynast	power, strength, strong	dynamic, dynasty
ec(o)	environment, house	ecology
elephan	elephant	elephantine
enni, annu	year	biennial, biannual
(s)ent, essent, essence	be	absent, present, essential
equ(i)	equal	equivalent, equator
erg	work	ergonomic
fac, fic, fact, fect, feit, fit	do, make	facilities, factory, benefit, confection

BASE	MEANING	EXAMPLE
fall, fals, fail, fault	false, mistake, fail	falsify, fallible, default
fel	cat	feline
fend, fens	strike	offend, defensive
fer, lat	to bear, bring, go	confer, collate
fess	speak	confess
fin, finit	end, limit, term	final, finite
flat	air, blow	inflate
flect, flex	bend	deflect, reflex
foc	focus	focal
for	hole, opening, doorway	perforated
forc, fort	power, strength, strong	enforce, fortify
form	form, shape	formal
fum	smoke, vapor	fumigate, perfume
funct	perform	function, defunct
fund, fus, found	pour, melt	foundry, refund, confuse
gam	marriage	polygamist
ge(o)	earth	geometry
gen, gener	be born, give birth, produce	genius, generation
ger, geront	elderly	geriatric, gerontology
glob	globe, sphere	globular, global
gnos, gnost	read, know	diagnosis, agnostic
gon	angle, corner	polygon, diagonal
grad, gress	step, go	gradual, congress
graph, gram	write, draw	graphite, telegram
greg	flock, group	gregarious, congregate
gyn, gynec	woman	gynecology
habit	dwell, keep	inhabit
hal(e)	breathe	inhale, halitosis

BASE	MEANING	EXAMPLE
haute	high	Terre Haute
(h)em, hemat	blood	anemia, hematology
hemer	day	ephemeral
hemi	one half	hemisphere
hepta	seven	heptagon
her, hes	stick, cling	coherent, adhesive
hexa	six	hexagon
(h)od	road	odometer, cathode
hor(o)	hour	horoscope
horr	frighten	horrify, horrible
hum	damp earth, moist	humus, humidity
human	human being, humankind	humane, humanity
hydr(o)	water	hydrant, hydrofoil
hypno	sleep	hypnosis
i, it	go	exit, transient
iatr	doctor	pediatrician
ig(u), ag, act	drive, go	ambiguous, agile, action
ject	throw, cast	eject, projectile
jur, juris	judge, oath	jury, jurisdiction
kilo	one thousand	kilogram
lab	take	syllable
labor	work	laborious
later	side	unilateral
lav	wash	lavatory
leg, lig, lect	pick, read	legible, eligible, collect
leo(n)	lion	leonine
libr	book	librarian
lingu	language	linguistics

BASE	MEANING	EXAMPLE
liter	letter	literature, illiterate
lith	stone	monolith
loc, locat	place	local, location
loqu, locut	speak, talk	elocution, eloquent
log	word, reason, study	logic
luc, lumin	light	lucid, luminous
lud, lus	play, trick	elude, illusion
lup	wolf	lupine
m(eridiem)	noon, midday	ante meridiem (a.m.)
magn	big	magnify
mal(e)	bad, evil, wrong	malevolent, malign
man, main	stay, remain	permanent, remain
man(u)	hand	manual
matr(i), matern	mother	matrimony, maternal
me(a)	wander, go	meander
medi	middle	medium
meter, metr(o), metr(i)	measure	centimeter, metronome, metric
milit	soldier, fight	military, militia
mill	one thousand	millimeter
mit, miss	send	missile, permit
mnem, mnes	memory	mnemonic, amnesia
mole	mass	molecule
mon(o)	alone, only, one	monologue
mor, mort	dead	moribund, mortal
mord, mors	bite	mordant, morsel
morph	shape, form	amorphous
mov, mot, mobil	move	move, promote, mobile

BASE	MEANING	EXAMPLE
mur	wall	mural
nat, natur, nasc	be born, give birth, produce	prenatal, natural, nascent
navig	sail	navigate
neo	new	neonatal
nihil	nothing	annihilate
noc, nox	harm	innocent, noxious
nomin	name	nominate
non, nov	nine	nonagon, November
noun	name	pronoun
nov	new	innovate
ocl(e), ocul	eye	monocle, binoculars
oct(a)	eight	octave
od	song	parody, ode
odont	tooth, teeth	periodontics
omni	all, every	omnipotent
onym	word, name	anonymous, pseudonym
orth(o)	straight	orthodontist
ov	sheep	ovine
pac	peace	pacify
pan	all, every	panacea, panoply
par, part	produce, beget	separate, postpartum
par, pear	appearance, seem	apparition, disappear
past, pastor	shepherd	pasture, pastoral
path	suffer, allow, feel	sympathy, pathology
pati, pass	suffer, allow, feel	patient, compassion
patr(i), patern	father	patriot, paternity
ped	foot, feet	pedal, impede
pel, puls, peal	drive, push	dispel, impulse, repeal

BASE	MEANING	EXAMPLE
pend, pens	weigh, hang, pay	pendant, suspense
penta	five	pentagon
petr	stone	petrify
phem	word, saying	euphemism
pher	bear, go	periphery
phil(o), phil(e)	love, friend	philodendron, anglophile
phon	voice, call, sound	telephone
photo	light	photograph
phragm	block, enclose	diaphragm
phyt	plant	neophyte
plac, pleas	calm, please	placate, pleasant
ple, plex, ply	fold, multiply	multiple, duplex, imply
plur, plus	more	plural, plus
pne, pneum	breathe	apnea, pneumonia
pol, polis	city	acropolis, political
pon, pos, posit, pound	put, place	components, positive, compound
port	carry	import
poss, pot	power	impossible, potentate
preci	price, value	appreciate, precious
pung, punct	pierce	puncture, pungent
quadr, quart	four	quadrant, quarter
quint	five	quintuplets
ras	scrape	abrasive, rash, erase
reg, rig, rect	straight, guide	regular, incorrigible, correct
rupt	break	interrupt, rupture
sanct(u)	holy, sacred	sanctuary
scend, scens	step, climb	descend, ascension

BASE	MEANING	EXAMPLE
scop	look, watch	microscope
scrib, script	write	scribe, scripture
sec, sect	cut, slice	secant, section
sed, sid, sess	sit, settle	sediment, reside, session
semi	one half, partial	semicircle
(s)ent, essent, essence	be	absent, present, essential
sent, sens	think, feel	sentence, sensation
seps, sept	infection	sepsis, antiseptic
sept(em), sept(a)	seven	septet, September
sequ, secut	follow	prosecute, sequel
serv, servat	save, keep, serve	servile, reservation
sex	six	sextet
sist	stand	persist, resistance
sit	food, feed	parasite
sol(i)	alone, only, one	soliloquy
solv, solut	free, loosen	dissolve, solution
somn(i)	sleep	somnambulist, somniloquist
son, sound	sound	resonate, resound
soph	wisdom, wise	philosophy
sorb	soak	absorb
spec, spic, spect	look, watch	specimen, conspicuous, spectacle
spir, (s)pir	breathe	perspire, expire
sta, stanc, stat	stand	stable, circumstance, static
stle, stol	send	epistle, apostolic
string, strict, strain	tie, bind, squeeze	restrain, restrict, stringent
stru, struct	build	construe, destructive
sui (swi)	pig, hog	swine

BASE	MEANING	EXAMPLE
tang, ting, tig, tact	touch	tangent, contingent, contiguous, intact
taph	grave, tomb	epitaph
taur	bull	taurus, Minotaur
techn	art, skill, fine craft	technique
tempor	time	temporary
ten, tin, tent, tain	hold	tenacious, continent, contents, retain, container
tend, tens, tent, tenu	stretch, thin	extend, tensile, tenuous, extent
terr, ter	land, ground, earth	inter, territory
test	witness	testify, testimony
tetra	four	tetrahedron
thanas, thanat	death	euthanasia
theater, theatr	theater, watch	theatrical, amphitheater
the(o)	god	atheist, theology
therm	heat	thermal
thes, thet	put, place	thesis, synthetic
tom	cut, slice	anatomy
ton	tone	monotonous
trac, tract	pull, drag, draw	trace, tractor
tri	three	tricycle, trident
trop	turn	tropics
trud, trus	push, thrust	intrude, protrusion
turb	shake, agitate	turbulence
uni, unit	one	unique, unite
urb, urban	city	suburban
urs	bear (the animal)	ursine, Ursa Major
val	be strong, be healthy	valid

BASE	MEANING	EXAMPLE
ven, vent	come	convene, advent
ventr(i)	belly	ventriloquist
ver	true, truth	veritable, very
verb	word	verbal, verbose
vert, vers	turn, change	adverse, advertise
vest	clothing	vestments
via	way, road	viaduct
vid, vis	see	video, visual
vigil	awake	vigilant
vit, viv	live, life	vital, revive
voc, vok, voice	voice, call, sound	vocal, revoke, invoice
vol	wish, will	volunteer
volv, volu, volut	roll	revolve, volume, revolution
vor	eat, devour	voracious
vulp	fox	vulpine
zo(o)	animal	zodiac, zoology

PREFIXES	MEANING	SAMPLE WORDS
a, ab, abs	away, from	avert, abduct, abstain
a, an	no, not, without	apnea, atheist, anemia
ad (+assimilated forms)	to, toward, add to	addition, aggregate, attract
ambi	around, on both sides	ambidextrous
amphi	around, on both sides	amphibian
ana	back, again, apart	analyze
ante	before	antecedent
anti, ant	against, opposite	antithesis, antonym
auto	self	autocrat, automobile
circu, circum	around	circuit, circumference

PREFIXES	MEANING	SAMPLE WORDS
co, con (+ assimilated forms)	with, together, very	cohesion, connect, compose, collection, correct
contra, contro, counter	against, opposite	contradict, controversy, counterpoint
de	down, off	demotion, descent
di, dis, dif	apart, in different directions, not	divert, dismiss, differ
dia	through, across, thorough	diameter, diagram, diagnosis
dys	bad, improper	dysfunction
e, ex, ef	out, out of, very	emit, effective, excel
em, en	in, on	emblem, encircle
epi	upon, to, add to	epidermis
eu, ev	good, well	eulogy, evangelist
hypo	below, under, up from under	hypothermia
in, im, il	not (negative)	inequity, improper, illegal
in, im, il	in, on, into (directional)	induct, impose, illuminate
infra	beneath	infrastructure
inter	between, among	intervene
mega, megalo	big	megachurch, megalomaniac
meta	across, change	metamorphosis
micro	small	microcosm
mis	wrongly	misinterpret, mistake
multi	many	multivitamin
ob (+ assimilated forms)	up against, in the way	obstruct, oppose, offend
para	alongside	paramedic, paranormal
per	through, thorough, wrongly	permeate, persecute
peri	around	perimeter
poly	many	polytheism
post	after	postpone

PREFIXES	MEANING	SAMPLE WORDS
pre	before	precedent
pro	forward, ahead, for	promotion, provoke
re	back, again	repel, revise
se	aside, apart	secession
sub (+assimilated forms)	below, under, up from under	submarine, suffer, suppose
super, sur	on top of, over, above	supersede, surreal
syn, sym, syl	with, together	synthesis, symphony, syllable
tele	far, from afar	telegram
trans, tra	across, change	transpose, travesty
un	not	unruly

SUFFIXES	MEANING	SAMPLE WORDS
able, ible	can or able to be done	portable, audible
ance, ancy, ence, ency	state or quality of	importance, hesitancy, patience, fluency
ant, ent	having the quality of	flagrant, potent
arch, archy	rule	monarch, oligarchy
arium, ary, orium, ory	place, room	aquarium, library, auditorium, laboratory
(as)tery, (e)tery	place	monastery, cemetery
ate	to make or do	equate
ation	the result of making or doing	incarnation
cracy	rule by	plutocracy
crat	ruler, one who believes in rule by	democrat
ectomy	surgical removal, "cutting out"	tonsillectomy
el, il, le	small	morsel, codicil, scruple
ella	small	umbrella
er	more	faster, bigger

SUFFIXES	MEANING	SAMPLE WORDS
er, or	someone who does, something that does	teacher, instructor
est	most	noblest, smartest
ful	full of	bountiful, plentiful
ify	to make	beautify
ion	state or act	construction
ism	belief, practice	monotheism
ist	one who believes or practices	artist, journalist
ive	tending to, inclined to	active, passive
ization	result or act of making	civilization
ize	to make	civilize
less	without	tireless
let, icle, cule	small	booklet, icicle, molecule
ly	in a way or manner	slowly
ologist	studier of, expert in	hematologist
ology	study of	biology
ose, ous, eous, ious	full of	verbose, populous, aqueous, spacious
phobe	one who fears	acrophobe
phobia	fear of	claustrophobia

Beyond Greek and Latin

The English language has certainly been influenced deeply by Greek and Latin. To this day, Greek and Latin continue to play a role in the introduction of new words into English, especially the new words that come from science and technology. Scientists and scholars will often lean on Greek and Latin when coming up with new words to express novel concepts and discoveries.

However, Greek and Latin are not the only languages that have had an impact on English. The chapter on the history of English and how we got here noted that whenever England was invaded by another group, the language of the new group had a significant influence on English. From the original Germanic invaders to the Vikings and the French, English has taken on words and characteristics of those people and their cultures.

The story of English would not be complete without an acknowledgment that English has been influenced by nearly every land, language, and culture with which it has come into contact. The following is a sampling of these words of influence.

AFRICAN		
aardvark	jazz	yarn
bongo	safari	zebra
gumbo	trek	zombie
impala	voodoo	

AMERICAN INDIAN		
caribou	hickory	opossum
chili	kayak	powwow
chocolate	moccasin	skunk
cougar	moose	squash
Eskimo	muskrat	tomahawk

ARABIC		
alcohol	bungalow	hazard
algebra	camphor	jasmine
apricot	chemistry	sofa
arsenal	cotton	tariff
artichoke	crimson	zenith
atlas	giraffe	zero

AUSTRALIAN (ABORIGINAL)		
dingo	koala	wombat
kangaroo	wallaby	yabber

CHINESE		
chow	ketchup	
ginkgo	kowtow	tea
ginseng	kung fu	wok
gung ho	sampan	

FRENCH		
accommodation	hospital	
accomplish	jacket	scholar
celebrate	porpoise	surgeon
female	rebound	unique
foliage	restaurant	vigorous
genius	resume	villain
gracious	savant	

GERMAN		
blitz	gestalt	pretzel
bratwurst	hinterland	sauerkraut
delicatessen	kindergarten	wanderlust
ersatz	poltergeist	zeitgeist

HEBREW		
amen	kibbutz	Satan
hallelujah	rabbi	schwa
jubilee	Sabbath	

INDIAN		
anaconda	ginger	nirvana
bangle	guru	orange
caravan	juggernaut	pundit
cot	loot	sandal
emerald	mantra	sentry

IRISH		
bard	dude	razz
bicker	giggle	scalawag
bother	guzzle	shindig
cantankerous	hoax	sneeze
cold turkey	pet	taunt
dork	phony	

ITALIAN		
bank	mandolin	porcelain
buffoon	medal	rotunda
bulletin	model	soda
coffee	paparazzi	solo
graffiti	pizza	virtue

JAPANESE		
futon	hooch	samurai
haiku	judo	soy
hibachi	karaoke	sushi
honcho	ninja	tycoon

SCANDINAVIAN (OLD NORSE, DANISH, NORWEGIAN, SWEDISH)		
birth	ombudsmen	slalom
blunder	ransack	tungsten
fjord	saga	wand
flounder	skin	wicker
guest	skirt	window
oaf	sky	ugly

SCOTTISH		
bog	glen	slob
caddy	golf	slogan
clan	plaid	smidgen
galore	rampage	trousers
glamour	slew	whiskey

SLAVIC (INCLUDING CZECH, POLISH, RUSSIAN, SLOVAK)		
babushka	intelligentsia	robot
bistro	kasha	ruble
dacha	kielbasa	sable
gulag	pogrom	steppe
howitzer	polka	vodka

SPANISH		
adios	embargo	silo
bonanza	guerrilla	tomato
cafeteria	mustang	tortilla
corral	patio	vamoose
coyote	renegade	vanilla

YIDDISH		
bagel	klutz	schmooze
blintz	kosher	shtick
glitch	nosh	

How to Teach Assimilation and Words with Two Prefixes

A Deep Dive into Assimilation

Some Latin prefixes occasionally change spelling to make words easier to pronounce. This is why some prefixes have multiple forms. For example, the prefix *con–* is found in various forms in the words *connect, combine, collect,* and *correct;* and variations of the prefix *ad–* are found in *advertise, attract, allusion,* and *affect.* Students do not need to learn each modification as a separate entity, since these changes follow a pattern that is recognizable and predictable: this is the phenomenon of assimilation. *Assimilation* simply means that some consonants change and become like ("similar to" = assimilate to) an adjacent consonant within a word.

You may wish to read the next few paragraphs to get the general idea. We will discuss the specific Latin prefixes that undergo assimilation (e.g., *con–, in–, ad–, dis–, sub–, ob–*). We will then follow with a useful teaching suggestion: make it as easy as 1, 2, 3. Students do not need to dwell on the technical term of *assimilation.* By looking at sample words (which are provided), they will get the point. If this concept is new to you as a teacher, the sample words will be likewise beneficial.

Assimilation is a common feature of many prefixes. Latin prefixes, like variant forms of Latin bases, undergo spelling changes with assimilation, but the meaning does not change. These spelling changes simply make words easier to pronounce. This is the principle of euphony (*phon* = "sound"; *eu–* = "good, well") or "sounding good." (Students do not need to dwell on this word; it suffices for them to be aware of it!) Although many consonants coexist in English words, some combinations are avoided. For example, English does not like the sound of a word such as *conlect,* so it changes the *n* of the prefix to match the first letter of the attached base. Thus, *conlect* becomes *collect.* Not only is it easier to say, but it also sounds better.

PARTIAL ASSIMILATION

Greek and Latin prefixes that end in consonants (e.g., Latin *con–* and *in–,* Greek *syn–*) may change when they attach to bases that begin with certain consonants. The final consonant of the prefix often changes into another consonant, facilitating pronunciation and enhancing euphony. In general, this change occurs only when the resulting consonant cluster would otherwise be difficult to pronounce or strike the ear as unpleasant.

In some words, the final *n* of a prefix can be softened into an *m*. This is especially common when the *n* of the prefix is followed by the consonants *b* or *p*:

con	+	bine	=	combine (double things "together")
con	+	pose	=	compose (put "together")
in	+	bibe	=	imbibe (drink "in")
in	+	possible	=	impossible ("not" possible)
syn	+	biotic	=	symbiotic (living "together")
syn	+	pathy	=	sympathy (feel "together")
syn	+	phony	=	symphony (sound "together")

The technical term for the modification of *n* into *m* in the above words is *retrogressive assimilation*. The initial *b* or *p* of the base looks "backward" (*retro–*) to the prefix and affects its pronunciation and spelling. It is not necessary to share such a technical term as "retrogressive assimilation" with students. We prefer to call it "partial assimilation." To keep things even simpler, we can just give this spelling rule to our students: before *b* and *p*, we change *n* to *m*.

FULL ASSIMILATION: DOUBLING CONSONANTS

When full assimilation occurs, the final *n* of the prefix changes into the same consonant as the first letter of the base. A doubled consonant always results.

con	+	lect	=	collect
con	+	motion	=	commotion
con	+	mit	=	commit
con	+	rect	=	correct
in	+	legal	=	illegal
in	+	legible	=	illegible
in	+	migrant	=	immigrant
syn	+	logism	=	syllogism

Again: when a prefix fully assimilates to match the first consonant of the base, we *always* observe a doubling of the consonant near the beginning of the word.

Now that we have seen how assimilation occurs with prefixes ending in *n*, let's look at the remaining few prefixes that end in other consonants. The prefix *ad–* ("to, toward, add to") has a very high degree of assimilation. Help students see that when they encounter a word beginning with *a* followed by a double consonant, they have found an assimilated *ad–* and should look for the meaning of "to, toward, add to" in the assimilated prefix.

ad	+	celerate	=	accelerate (to "add to" speed)
ad	+	fect	=	affect (to do something "to")
ad	+	gravate	=	aggravate (to "add to" the weight of a problem)
ad	+	legiance	=	allegiance (loyalty "to" a country or cause)
ad	+	pendix	=	appendix (a section "added to" the end of a book)
ad	+	rogant	=	arrogant ("adding to" one's sense of importance)
ad	+	similate	=	assimilate (to liken one thing "to" another)
ad	+	tract	=	attract (to draw something "to" or "toward" itself)

It is important to note that the prefix *a–*, *ab–*, *abs–* ("away, from"), found in words such as *abduct*, *absent*, *abstain*, and *abhor*, does **not** assimilate. Some students may confuse this prefix with its opposite, *ad–*. You may want to remind students that *ad–* always has a *d* or a double consonant, but the prefix *a–*, *ab–*, *abs–* never does.

The Latin prefix *dis–*, *di–* assimilates into *dif–* only when the base begins with *f*. Assimilated examples are *different*, *diffuse*, *diffract*, and *difficult*. Unassimilated examples of this prefix include *distribute*, *disqualify*, *disposal*, *divest*, *divulge*, and *direct*. The prefix *e–*, *ex–* exhibits the same pattern: it assimilates into *ef–* only when the base begins with *f*. Assimilated examples include *effect*, *efficient*, *effort*, and *effusive*. Unassimilated examples of this prefix include *eruption*, *erode*, *educate*, *exit*, *excel*, *exceed*, *excise*, and *expel*.

The Latin prefix *ob–* ("up against") also assimilates into many spellings that are easily recognizable. When this prefix can be easily pronounced with the base that follows, it retains its spelling as *ob–*. Thus, we encounter such words as *obstruction* (something "built in the way" of something else), *objection* (one statement or opinion "thrown up against" another), and *obnoxious* (noticeably "harmful" or bothersome, with the sense of striking "up against" the observer).

When *ob–* assimilates, the final *b* of the prefix changes into the first consonant of the base. The result is always a doubling of the consonant after the initial *o*. To "divide and conquer," students simply divide between the doubled consonants and translate the prefix into *ob–*. With practice, students will readily recognize that most words beginning with *opp–*, *off–*, and *occ–* contain an assimilated *ob–*.

ob	+	pose	=	oppose ("place" "up against")
ob	+	fer	=	offer ("bring" "up against")
ob	+	currence	=	occurrence (a "running" "up against")
ob	+	press	=	oppress ("press" "up against" and crush)

The prefix *sub–*, like the prefix *ob–*, ends in the consonant *b*. When *sub–* assimilates, it displays the same pattern as *ob–*. Words beginning with *supp–*, *suff–*, and *succ–* contain an assimilated *sub–*. Students should look for a doubled consonant after *su–* and translate the prefix into *sub–*.

sub	+	fer	=	suffer ("bear" "up from under")
sub	+	fuse	=	suffuse ("pour" or flush "up from under")
sub	+	ceed	=	succeed ("come, move" "up from under")
sub	+	port	=	support ("carry" "up from under")
sub	+	press	=	suppress ("press" "below" and keep "under")

Teaching Assimilation: As Easy As 1, 2, 3

For teachers who feel that students may benefit from a fuller explanation of assimilation (without the technical terminology!), we suggest three simple steps. These steps rely on a few sample words to walk students through the spelling process. These steps also utilize one of the first strategies students learned as beginning readers: saying the words out loud.

Because euphony is the driving principle, it is important that students sound out the words with the teacher. For each step, first write the original prefix, and then modify the spelling to make the word easier to say.

Step 1: Present and pronounce a word with an unassimilated prefix.

Step 2: Pronounce a word with the same prefix that is only partially assimilated.

Step 3: Pronounce a word with a fully assimilated prefix, spelled with a doubled consonant.

Here are some suggestions using some of the most frequently assimilated prefixes:

PREFIX	STEP 1	STEP 2	STEP 3
(negative) in–	*invisible* ("not" able to be seen; easy to pronounce as is)	*impossible* ("not" possible; "inpossible" is hard to pronounce)	*illegal* ("not" legal; "inlegal" is hard to pronounce)
(directional) in–	*incision* (a cut made "into" a surface; easy to pronounce as is)	*import* (carry goods "into" a country; "inport" is hard to pronounce)	*immerse* (plunge "into" water; "inmerse" is hard to pronounce)
con–	*convention* (people coming "together" in a large meeting; easy to pronounce as is)	*combine* (double or group things "together"; "conbine" is hard to pronounce)	*collection* (a gathering "together" of items; "conlection" is hard to pronounce)

For the prefixes *ad–*, *sub–*, and *ob–*, only two steps are needed (one for the unassimilated prefix and one for the assimilated prefix, always resulting in a doubled consonant):

PREFIX	STEP 1	STEP 2
ad–	*advertise* (turn public attention "toward" a product; easy to pronounce)	*attract* (draw "to, toward" something; "adtract" is hard to pronounce)
sub–	*submarine* (vessel that travels "below" sea level; easy to pronounce)	*support* (carry and hold "up from under"; "subport" is hard to pronounce
ob–	*observe* (keep a close watch "up against" something; easy to pronounce)	*oppose* (place oneself "up against" a rival; "obpose" is hard to pronounce)

With each prefix and sample word, ask students to sound out the words with you. They will see how hard the unassimilated prefixes are to pronounce. Then, go back to the written form, emphasizing that a double consonant near the beginning of the word is almost always the sign of a prefix they have studied!

How to "Divide and Conquer" Words with Two Prefixes

One final issue dealing with prefixes remains: how to "divide and conquer" words with two prefixes. Here are some examples:

disconnect (*dis–* + *con–*)

reproduce (*re–* + *pro–*)

misconstrue (*mis–* + *con–*)

decompose (*de–* + partially assimilated *con–*)

incorruptible (*in–* + assimilated *con–*)

unattractive (*un–* + assimilated *ad–*)

irreversible (assimilated *in–* + *re–*)

The procedure for "dividing and conquering" these words is similar to the procedure for words with one prefix. Because words with two prefixes are longer, it may take more time for students to zero in on the base or the root word. In general, we suggest the following tips, keeping in mind that the definition of the word must always make sense.

In words beginning with two prefixes, the initial prefix almost always attaches to a readily recognizable word (e.g., *dis–* + *connect*, *re–* + *produce*). When we "divide and conquer," we tell students to remove the first prefix and see whether they recognize the rest of the word.

In addition, words with double prefixes fall into two categories:

- The initial prefix is a negating prefix (*de–*, *dis–*, *in–*, *un–*, all meaning "not"). This category includes words beginning with *mis–*, which means "wrong, wrongly." Notice, in these pairs of words, how the double-prefix word negates the first:

segregate	desegregate
respectful	disrespectful
precise	imprecise
dependent	independent
comfortable	uncomfortable
pronounce	mispronounce (pronounce "wrongly")

- Or the initial prefix is *re–*, meaning "again." Notice, in these pairs of words, how the double-prefix word repeats the action implied in the first:

construction	reconstruction
install	reinstall
submit	resubmit

Despite their length, double-prefix words are not as complicated as they look. Divide and conquer!

Professional Development Ideas

Each chapter in this book explores a different dimension of vocabulary study based on Greek and Latin roots. Many of the ideas in these chapters can be adapted to fit each classroom's unique needs. Use the following questions and suggestions for personal reflection and professional conversation with colleagues.

1. Think back to the vocabulary instruction that characterized your own school years. What were you asked to do with words? Try to identify at least three activities that stand out. How effective were they? Did they lead to word learning?

    Share your memories with one another by comparing the activities and their effectiveness. Are there any similarities? If so, can you make any generalizations about vocabulary teaching and learning in American classrooms?

2. If you could make three changes to your vocabulary program, what would they be? Select the most important change, and make an action plan for achieving it.

    Share your plans with one another. Give one another feedback. Make sure to jot down any suggestions that seem particularly good.

3. If you or your colleagues are currently using a vocabulary program, evaluate it. Identify its strengths and weaknesses. The following questions (adapted from Newton et al. 2008) may assist you as you analyze and discuss your findings:

    -   What is the logic inherent in the words selected for focus? Are the words appropriate for your students' developmental levels?

    -   Do your students find the activities engaging?

    -   Do the activities help your students build and deepen their conceptual knowledge?

    -   Do students learn and apply word analysis strategies, particularly the study of word roots and context clues?

    -   Do activities feature student discussion about vocabulary?

    -   Are there opportunities for students to deepen their understanding of how words "work" through written or oral reflection?

    -   Are whole-group, small-group, and individual activities appropriate?

    -   Do activities promote interest in words? Are activities game-like and playful?

    -   Does the program offer strategies to differentiate instruction so that all learners can grow?

- Are a variety of scaffolding practices available for students who need it?
- Is the amount of time per day appropriate (10–15 minutes daily)?
- Is the overall instructional routine appropriate?
- Does the program fit well with the rest of your literacy curriculum?
- Are assessment ideas offered?

4. Identify a student whose vocabulary is particularly good. Think about why that student stands out, and make a list of observable indicators. Now, identify a student whose vocabulary is limited. Make a second list of their observable indicators.

Share your lists with one another. Are there similarities among the indicators you have listed? If so, discuss how you might use some of the ideas in this book to differentiate instruction for students with advanced or limited vocabularies.

5. What key mathematics, social studies, and science concepts are you responsible for teaching? Make a list of key vocabulary words in each area. Identify 5 to 10 of the most common prefixes and bases in those words. Develop an action plan for teaching those roots.

Share your list of roots and your action plan with colleagues. Give one another feedback. Make sure to jot down any suggestions that seem particularly good.

6. Even though their English language skills are often limited, students who speak a language other than English can enhance the vocabulary learning experience of all students. Think about the EL students in your classroom. What first languages do they speak? What cultural backgrounds do they represent? What unique contributions can they make to vocabulary and root study?

Share your ideas with colleagues. Discuss how your EL students' linguistic and cultural strengths might be used to highlight some of the ideas in this book.

7. Chapter 6 presents several classroom-tested "practice activities" to support vocabulary development. Identify two or three of those activities that are especially well suited to your students. Make concrete plans to implement each one by considering why, when, and how you will use it.

Share the activities and plans with your colleagues. Give one another feedback. Make sure to jot down any suggestions that seem particularly good.

8. Throughout the book, you read vignettes of teachers and students engaged in exemplary vocabulary instruction. Below are several guidelines exemplified in these vignettes. Select one of them, and brainstorm new activities you might implement to enhance your vocabulary program in this area:

- Tuck "word talk" into all lessons.
- Encourage students to become word sleuths.
- Teach the word-analysis strategy of "divide and conquer."
- Provide direct instruction for key vocabulary.
- Share your own love of words with your students.
- Make time for word play.
- Promote wide reading on a variety of topics.
- Share your ideas with one another. Give one another feedback. Make sure to jot down any suggestions that seem particularly good.

9. How might you connect your vocabulary and word-study program to the homes of your students? What would you communicate to parents? What would you ask parents to do in order to support the vocabulary and word study in your classroom? Make notes about your ideas. Then, share them with colleagues.

10. Make a list of the vocabulary assessment activities you currently employ. Evaluate each of these assessment practices:
    - Useful for assessing active vocabulary (speaking and writing)
    - Useful for assessing passive vocabulary (listening and reading)
    - Useful for assessing vocabulary growth
    - Useful for student self-assessment

    Identify weaknesses in your vocabulary assessment strategies. Share results with your colleagues. Seek their ideas about strengthening aspects of your assessments. Make plans to strengthen them.

11. Do you currently use electronic or print dictionaries in classroom instruction? After reading this book, what are some new ways you might use the dictionary to encourage your students' interest in words? Brainstorm ideas with one another, and jot down those that seem best suited to your classroom needs.

12. Appendices A and B provide web-based and print resources for you and for your students. Review the resources, and choose one student resource and one teacher resource that you think may be particularly useful.

Explore those resources, and report your findings to colleagues. Describe the content, and explain how you might use them. Note any resources they report on that seem well suited to your instructional needs.

Glossary

active vocabulary—the words we know well enough to use in speaking or writing

affix—a morpheme that changes the meaning or function of a root to which it is attached; includes prefixes and suffixes

assimilate—to make a sound similar or identical to an adjacent sound in order to ease pronunciation

base—a word or word part to which affixes may be added to create related words; also called a *root* or *base word*

cognate—a word related in form and meaning to another word. This relationship is the result of the words sharing a common source; also called a *root family*

colloquial/colloquialism—informal or spoken language

compound word—a combination of two or more words that functions as a single unit

context—the words or phrases adjacent to another language unit

decontextualized—having the context taken away

derivative—a word formed by adding an affix; a related word

figurative meaning—a word has a figurative meaning when it stands for or represents an idea; can be abstract or symbolic

lingua franca—a common language used by diverse cultures in shared communication

literal meaning—a word has a literal meaning when it represents something concrete or physical

metacognition—an awareness and knowledge of one's own thought processes; applied to reading, this ordinarily refers to the reader's ability to monitor reading and apply fix-up strategies, should they be necessary

metalinguistics—an awareness and knowledge of language as an object itself

metaphor—a type of figurative language in which a comparison is implied but not directly stated

morpheme—the smallest unit of language that carries meaning

morphology—the study of the forms and structure of words

neologism—a new word

passive vocabulary—the words we understand in reading or in listening

phoneme—the smallest unit of language that carries sound

phonogram—a sound-based word pattern; also called a *rime* or *word family*; knowledge of individual phonograms allows readers to decode or "sound out" words that contain those phonograms

polysemy—words that have more than one meaning

prefix—an affix attached before a base word

rime—the part of a syllable that begins with the vowel and contains any letters in the syllable that come after the vowel; a rime is a sound-based word pattern; also called a *phonogram* or *word family*

Romance languages—"any of the Italic Indo-European languages derived from Latin in the Middle Ages; chiefly French, Spanish, Italian, Portuguese, and Romanian" (Harris and Hodges 1995, 222)

root—"the basic part of a word that usually carries the main component of meaning and that cannot be further identified without loss of identity" (Harris and Hodges 1995, 222)

root family—also called a *cognate*; collection of words that contain a common root and have a shared meaning

semantic context—the meaning of words or phrases adjacent to another language unit

suffix—an affix attached after a base word

syllable—a pronunciation portion of a word having one and only one vowel sound

syntactic context—the word order (grammar) of words or phrases adjacent to another language unit

word family—a sound-based word pattern; also called a *phonogram* or *rime*; words belonging to a word family (e.g. *–at: cat, fat, scat*) usually have similar sound representations

References Cited

Allington, Richard L., and Patricia M. Cunningham. 2001. *Schools That Work: Where All Children Read and Write*. 2nd ed. New York: HarperCollins.

Ayers, Donald M. 1986. *English Words from Latin and Greek Elements*. Tucson, AZ: University of Arizona Press.

Banchero, Stephanie. 2013. "Students Fall Flat in Vocabulary Test." *The Wall Street Journal*, January 4, 2013. http://www.wsj.com/articles/SB10001424127887323316804578163213067015532.

Banks, Kate. 2006. *Max's Words*. New York: Farrar, Straus, and Giroux.

Baumann, James F., George Font, Elizabeth Carr Edwards, and Eileen Boland. 2005. "Strategies for Teaching Middle-Grade Students to Use Word-Part and Context Clues to Expand Reading Vocabulary." In *Teaching and Learning Vocabulary: Bringing Research to Practice*, edited by Elfrieda H. Hiebert and Michael L. Kamil, 179–205. Mahwah, NJ: Erlbaum.

Baumann, James, and Michael Graves. 2010. "What Is Academic Vocabulary?" *Journal of Adolescent and Adult Literacy* 54, no. 1 (September): 4–12.

Baumann, James, Edward Kame'enui, and Gwynne Ash. 2003. "Research on Vocabulary Instruction: Voltaire Redux." In *Handbook of Research on Teaching the English Language Arts*. 2nd ed., edited by James Flood, Douglas Fisher, Diane Lapp, James R. Squire, and Julie Jensen, 752–785. Hillsdale, NJ: Erlbaum.

Bear, Donald, Marcia R. Invernizzi, Shane R. Templeton, and Francine Johnston. 2000. *Words Their Way: Word Study for Phonics, Vocabulary, & Spelling Instruction*. 2nd ed. Upper Saddle River, NJ: Prentice Hall.

Biemiller, Andrew. 2005. "Size and Sequence in Vocabulary Development: Implications for Choosing Words for Primary Grade Vocabulary Instruction." In *Teaching and Learning Vocabulary: Bringing Research to Practice*, edited by Elfrieda H. Hiebert and Michael L. Kamil, 223–242. Mahwah, NJ: Erlbaum.

Blachowicz, Camille L. Z., and Peter J. Fisher. 2002. *Teaching Vocabulary in All Classrooms*. 2nd ed. Upper Saddle River, NJ: Prentice Hall.

———. 2006. *Teaching Vocabulary in All Classrooms*. 3rd ed. Upper Saddle River, NJ: Prentice Hall.

———. 2015. *Teaching Vocabulary in All Classrooms*. 5th ed. New York: Pearson.

Blachowicz, Camille L. Z., Peter J. Fisher, Donna Ogle, and Susan Watts-Taffe. 2006. "Vocabulary: Questions from the Classroom." *Reading Research Quarterly* 41, no. 4 (October): 524–538.

Blachowicz, Camille L. Z., and Connie Obrochta. 2005. "Vocabulary Visits: Virtual Field Trips for Content Vocabulary Development." *The Reading Teacher* 59, no. 3 (November): 262–268.

Bravo, Marco A., and Gina N. Cervetti. 2008. "Teaching Vocabulary through Text and Experience in Content Areas." In *What Research Has to Say about Vocabulary Instruction*, edited by Alan E. Farstrup and S. Jay Samuels, 130–149. Newark, DE: International Reading Association.

Brook, Donna. 1998. *The Journey of English*. New York: Clarion Books.

Brunner, B. L. 2004. *Word Empire: A Utilitarian Approach to Word Power*. 2nd ed. Star Nemeton Educational Innovations.

Butler, Frances A., Robin Stevens, and Martha Castellon. 2007. "ELLs and Standardized Assessments: The Interaction between Language Proficiency and Standardized Tests." In *The Language Demands of School: Putting Academic English to the Test*, edited Alison L. Bailey, 27–49. New Haven, CT: Yale University Press.

Chandler, Richard E., and Kessel Schwartz. 1961. *A New History of Spanish Literature*. Baton Rouge, LA: Louisiana State University Press.

Cruz, Gilbert. 2007. "10 Best Buzzwords of 2007." *Time*, December 10, 2007.

Cunningham, Anne E. 2005. "Vocabulary Growth through Independent Reading and Reading Aloud to Children." In *Teaching and Learning Vocabulary: Bringing Research to Practice*, edited by Elfrieda H. Hiebert and Michael L. Kamil, 45–68. Mahwah, NJ: Erlbaum.

Cunningham, Patricia M. 1998. "The Multisyllabic Word Dilemma: Helping Students Build Meaning, Spell, and Read 'Big' Words." *Reading and Writing Quarterly* 14 (2): 189–218.

Cunningham, James W., and David W. Moore. 1993. "The Contributions of Understanding Academic Vocabulary to Answering Comprehension Questions." *Journal of Reading Behavior* 25 (2): 171–189.

Fry, Edward. 1998. "The Most Common Phonograms." *The Reading Teacher* 51 (7): 620–622.

Graves, Michael F., and Jill Fitzgerald. 2006. "Effective Vocabulary Instruction for English-Language Learners." In *The Vocabulary-Enriched Classroom*, edited by Cathy Collins Block and John N. Mangieri, 118–37. New York: Scholastic.

Graves, Michael F., and Susan M. Watts-Taffe. 2002. "The Place of Word Consciousness in a Research-Based Vocabulary Program." In *What Research Has to Say about Reading Instruction*, 3rd ed., edited by Alan E. Farstrup and S. Jay Samuels, 140–165. Newark, DE: International Reading Association.

Green, Tamara M. 2008. *The Greek & Latin Roots of English*. 4th ed. Lanham, MD: Rowman & Littlefield.

Harmon, Janis M., Karen D. Wood, and Wanda B. Hedrick. 2008. "Vocabulary Instruction in Middle and Secondary Content Classrooms: Understandings and Directions from Research." In *What Research Has to Say about Vocabulary Instruction*, edited by Alan E. Farstrup and S. Jay Samuels, 150–181. Newark, DE: International Reading Association.

Harris, Theodore L., and Richard E. Hodges. 1995. *The Literacy Dictionary: The Vocabulary of Reading and Writing*. Newark, DE: International Reading Association.

Hart, Betty, and Todd R. Risley. 1995. *Meaningful Differences in the Everyday Experiences of Young American Children*. Baltimore: Brookes.

———. 2003. "The Early Catastrophe. The 30 Million Word Gap." *American Educator* 27, no. 1 (Spring): 4–9.

Haynes, Judie. 2007. *Getting Started with English Language Learners*. Alexandria, VA: Association for Supervision and Curriculum Development.

Hewitt, Sally. 1995. *The Romans*. London: Franklin Watts.

Horace. 2014. *Satires; Epistles; The Art of Poetry*. Cambridge, MA: Harvard University Press.

Hiebert, Elfrieda H., and Shira Lubliner. 2008. "The Nature, Learning and Instruction of General Academic Vocabulary." In *What Research Has to Say about Vocabulary Instruction*, edited by Alan E. Farstrup and S. Jay Samuels, 106–129. Newark, DE: International Reading Association.

Hoyt, Linda. 1999. *Revisit, Reflect, Retell: Strategies for Improving Reading Comprehension*. Portsmouth, NH: Heinemann.

Kamil, Michael, and Elfrieda Hiebert. 2005. *Teaching and Learning vocabulary: Bringing Research to Practice*. Mahwah, NJ: Erlbaum.

Lakoff, George, and Mark Johnson. 1980. *Metaphors We Live By*. Chicago: University of Chicago Press.

Lehr, Fran, Jean Osborn, and Elfrieda H. Hiebert. 2004. "A Focus on Vocabulary." *Research-Based Practices in Early Reading Series*. Honolulu, HI: Pacific Resources for Education and Learning.

Martin, Jacqueline Briggs. 1998. *Snowflake Bentley*. Boston: Houghton Mifflin.

Marzano, Robert J., Debra J. Pickering, and Jane E. Pollock. 2001. *Classroom Instruction That Works: Research-Based Strategies for Increasing Student Achievement*. Alexandria, VA: Association for Supervision and Curriculum Development.

Mattson, Mark P. 2014. "Superior Pattern Processing Is the Essence of the Evolved Human Brain." *Frontiers in Neuroscience* 8: article 265. https://doi.org/10.3389/fnins.2014.00265.

McCrum, Robert, William Cran, and Robert MacNeil. 1987. *The Story of English*. New York: Penguin Books.

Merriam-Webster's Collegiate Dictionary. 11th ed. 2003. Springfield, MA: Merriam-Webster, Inc.

Merriam-Webster's Online Dictionary. http://www.merriam-webster.com (accessed March 2019).

Nagy, William E. 1988. *Teaching Vocabulary to Improve Reading Comprehension*. Urbana, IL: National Council of Teachers of English.

Nagy, William E., and Richard C. Anderson. 1984. "How Many Words Are There in Printed School English?" *Reading Research Quarterly* 19, no. 3 (Spring): 304–330.

Nagy, William E., Georgia Earnest García, Aydın Durgunoğlu, and Barbara Hancin-Bhatt. 1993. "Spanish-English Bilingual Children's Use and Recognition of Cognates in English Reading." *Journal of Reading Behavior* 25 (3): 241–259.

Nagy, William E., and Judith A. Scott. 2000. "Vocabulary Processes." In *Handbook of Reading Research Volume III*, edited by Michael L. Kamil, Peter B. Mosenthal, P. David Pearson, and Rebecca Barr, 269–284. Mahwah, NJ: Erlbaum.

Nation, I. S. P. 2001. *Learning Vocabulary in Another Language*. Cambridge, UK: Cambridge University Press.

National Center for Education Statistics. 2015. *The Nation's Report Card, 2015: Vocabulary*. Accessed November 15, 2017. http://www.nationsreportcard.gov/reading_2013/vocabulary /#knowledge

National Reading Panel. 2000. *Report of the National Reading Panel: Teaching Children to Read: Report of the Subgroups*. Washington, DC: U.S. Government Printing Office.

Newton, Evangeline, Nancy Padak, and Timothy Rasinski. 2008. *Evidence-Based Instruction in Reading: A Professional Development Guide to Vocabulary Instruction*. Boston: Pearson.

Newton, Joanna. 2018. "Teachers as Learners: The Impact of Teachers' Morphological Awareness on Vocabulary Instruction." *Education Sciences* 8, (4): 161–170.

———. 2018. "Teachers' experiences with professional development and a morphological approach to vocabulary instruction" (Doctoral dissertation). Retrieved from ProQuest. (10792776.)

Online Etymology Dictionary. http://www.etymonline.com (accessed March 2020).

Parish, Peggy. 1995. *Amelia Bedelia's Treasury*. New York: Harper Collins.

Pearson, P. David, Elfrieda Hiebert, and Michael Kamil. 2007. "Vocabulary Assessment: What We Know and What We Need to Learn." *Reading Research Quarterly* 42, no. 2 (Spring): 282–296.

Pérez, Bertha. 2004. "Language, Literacy, and Biliteracy." In *Sociocultural Contexts of Language and Literacy*. 2nd ed, edited by Bertha Pérez, 25–56. Mahwah, NJ: Erlbaum.

Rasinski, Timothy. 2001. *Making and Writing Words (Grades 3–6)*. Greensboro, NC: Carson-Dellosa Publishing.

Rasinski, Timothy, and Nancy Padak. 2013. *From Phonics to Fluency*. 3rd ed. Boston: Pearson.

Rasinski, Timothy, Nancy Padak, and Gay Fawcett. 2010. *Teaching Children Who Find Reading Difficult*. 4th ed. Boston: Allyn and Bacon.

Rasinski, Timothy, Nancy Padak, and Joanna Newton. 2017. "The Roots of Comprehension." *Educational Leadership* 74 (5): 41–45.

Rasinski, Timothy, Nancy Padak, Rick M. Newton, and Evangeline Newton. 2019. *Building Vocabulary from Word Roots*. 2nd ed. Huntington Beach, CA: Teacher Created Materials.

Reutzel, D. Ray, and Robert Cooter. 2015. *Teaching Children to Read: The Teacher Makes the Difference*. 7th ed. New York: Pearson.

Reutzel, D. Ray, and Parker Fawson. 2002. *Your Classroom Library: New Ways to Give It More Teaching Power*. New York: Scholastic.

Roosevelt, Franklin D. 1941. Quote accessed at http://www.archives.gov/education/lessons /day-of-infamy.

Schotter, Roni. 2006. *The Boy Who Loved Words*. New York: Schwartz Wade Books.

Shulman, Mark. 2006. *Mom and Dad Are Palindromes*. San Francisco: Chronicle Books.

Silverstein, Shel. 2005. *Where the Sidewalk Ends*. New York: Scholastic, Inc.

Stahl, Steven. 1986. "Three Principles of Effective Vocabulary Instruction." *Journal of Reading* 29 (7): 662–671.

Stahl, Steven, and Marilyn Fairbanks. 1986. "The Effects of Vocabulary Instruction: A Model-Based Meta-Analysis." *Review of Educational Research* 56, no.1 (Spring): 72–110.

Sweet, Anne Polselli, and Catherine E. Snow, eds. 2003. *Rethinking Reading Comprehension*. New York: Guilford Press.

Templeton, Shane, and Darrell Morris. 2000. Reconceptualizing spelling development and instruction. In *Handbook of Reading Research Volume III*, edited by Michael L. Kamil, Peter B. Mosenthal, P. David Pearson, and Rebecca Barr. Reprinted: *Reading Online* 5 no. 3 (October).

Twain, Mark. Letter to George Bainton, October 15, 1888.

Weaver, Constance. 2002. *Reading Process and Practice*. 3rd ed. Portsmouth, NH: Heinemann.

Wexler, Natalie. 2019. *The Knowledge Gap: The Hidden Cause of America's Broken Education System—and How to Fix It*. New York: Avery.

White, Thomas G., Joanne Sowell, and Alice Yanagihara. 1989. "Teaching Elementary Students to Use Word-Part Clues." *The Reading Teacher* 42, no. 4 (January): 302–308.

Worthington, Denice, and I. S. P. Nation. 1996. "Using Texts to Sequence the Introduction of New Vocabulary in an EAP Course." *RELC Journal* 27, no. 2 (December): 1–11.